French Games pack

CONTENTS
Bonne Idée
Loto Français
Jouons Tous Ensemble

We hope you and your pupils enjoy using this compendium of 3 books. Brilliant Publications publishes many other books for teaching modern foreign languages. To find out more details on any of the titles listed below, please go to our website: www.brilliantpublications.co.uk.

100+ Fun Ideas for Practising Modern Foreign Languages in the Primary Classroom	978-1-903853-98-6
More Fun Ideas for Advancing Modern Foreign Languages in the Primary Classroom	978-1-905780-72-3
Chantez Plus Fort!	978-1-903853-37-5
Hexagonie Part 1	978-1-905780-59-4
Hexagonie Part 2	978-1-905780-18-1
C'est Français!	978-1-903853-02-3
J'aime Chanter!	978-1-905780-11-2
J'aime Parler!	978-1-905780-12-9
French Pen Pals Made Easy	978-1-905780-10-5
French Festivals and Traditions	978-1-905780-44-0
Loto Français	978-1-905780-45-7
Unforgettable French (2nd edition)	978-1-78317-093-7
¡Es Español!	978-1-903853-64-1
Juguemos Todos Juntos	978-1-903853-95-5
¡Vamos a Cantar!	978-1-905780-13-6
Spanish Pen Pals Made Easy	978-1-905780-42-6
Lotto en Español	978-1-905780-47-1
Spanish Festivals and Traditions	978-1-905780-53-2
Buena Idea	978-1-905780-63-1
Das ist Deutsch	978-1-905780-15-0
Wir Spielen Zusammen	978-1-903853-97-9
German Pen Pals Made Easy	978-1-905780-43-3
Deutsch-Lotto	978-1-905780-46-4
German Festivals and Traditions	978-1-905780-52-5
Gute Idee	978-1-905780-65-5
Giochiamo Tutti Insieme	978-1-903853-96-2
Lotto in Italiano	978-1-905780-48-8
Buon'Idea (2nd edition)	978-0-85747-696-8

Published by Brilliant Publications
Unit 10
Sparrow Hall Farm
Edlesborough
Dunstable
Bedfordshire
LU6 2ES, UK

Website: www.brilliantpublications.co.uk

General information enquiries:
Tel: 01525 222292

The name Brilliant Publications and the logo are registered trademarks.

Front cover designed by Brilliant Publications

Printed book ISBN: 978-0-85747-946-4
E-book ISBN: 978-0-85747-947-1

First printed and published in the UK in 2021

See the copyright pages of each individual book for the rights of the authors.

See the copyright pages of each individual book to ascertain the restrictions on photocopying pages.

Bonne Idée

Time saving resources and ideas for busy French teachers

Nicolette Hannam and Michelle Williams

We hope you and your pupils enjoy using this book. Brilliant Publications publishes many other books for teaching modern foreign languages. To find out more details on any of the titles listed below, please log onto our website: www.brilliantpublications.co.uk.

100+ Fun Ideas for Practising Modern Foreign Languages in the Primary Classroom	978-1-903853-98-6
More Fun Ideas for Advancing Modern Foreign Languages in the Primary Classroom	978-1-905780-72-3
Chantez Plus Fort!	978-1-903853-37-5
Hexagonie Part 1	978-1-905780-59-4
Hexagonie Part 2	978-1-905780-18-1
Jouons Tous Ensemble	978-1-903853-81-8
C'est Français!	978-1-903853-02-3
J'aime Chanter!	978-1-905780-11-2
J'aime Parler!	978-1-905780-12-9
French Pen Pals Made Easy	978-1-905780-10-5
Loto Français	978-1-905780-45-7
French Festivals and Traditions	978-1-905780-44-0
Unforgettable French (2nd edition)	978-1-78317-093-7
¡Es Español!	978-1-903853-64-1
Juguemos Todos Juntos	978-1-903853-95-5
¡Vamos a Cantar!	978-1-905780-13-6
Spanish Pen Pals Made Easy	978-1-905780-42-6
Lotto en Español	978-1-905780-47-1
Spanish Festivals and Traditions	978-1-905780-53-2
Buena Idea	978-1-905780-63-1
Das ist Deutsch	978-1-905780-15-0
Wir Spielen Zusammen	978-1-903853-97-9
German Pen Pals Made Easy	978-1-905780-43-3
Deutsch-Lotto	978-1-905780-46-4
German Festivals and Traditions	978-1-905780-52-5
Gute Idee	978-1-905780-65-5
Giochiamo Tutti Insieme	978-1-903853-96-2
Lotto in Italiano	978-1-905780-48-8
Buon'Idea (2nd edition)	978-0-85747-696-8

Published by Brilliant Publications
Unit 10
Sparrow Hall Farm
Edlesborough
Dunstable
Bedfordshire
LU6 2ES, UK

Website: www.brilliantpublications.co.uk

General information enquiries:
Tel: 01525 222292

The name Brilliant Publications and the logo are registered trademarks.

Written by Nicolette Hannam and Michelle Williams
Illustrated by Catherine Ward
Designed by Bookcraft Ltd
Front cover designed by Brilliant Publications

© Text Nicolette Hannam and Michelle Williams 2009
© Design Brilliant Publications 2009

Printed ISBN: 978-1-905780-62-4
ebook ISBN: 978-0-85747-000-3

First printed and published in the UK in 2009

The right of Nicolette Hannam and Michelle Williams to be identified as the authors of this work has been asserted by themselves in accordance with the Copyright, Designs and Patents Act 1988.

Pages 5–148 may be photocopied by individual teachers acting on behalf of the purchasing institution for classroom use only, without permission from the publisher and without declaration to the Copyright Licensing Agency or Publishers' Licensing Services. The materials may not be reproduced in any other form or for any other purpose without the prior permission of the publisher.

Contents

Les chiffres	The numbers	5
Les jours	The days	11
Les mois	The months	16
Ma famille	My family	22
Les couleurs	The colours	28
As-tu un animal?	Do you have a pet?	36
La salle de classe	The classroom	42
Au collège	School subjects	50
Bon appétit	Food	56
Quel temps fait-il?	What's the weather like?	64
Le corps	The body	70
Mes passe-temps	My hobbies	78
Les vêtements	Clothes	86
En ville	In the town	94
Ma maison	My house	102
Joyeux Noël	Happy Christmas	110
Saint-Valentin	Valentine's Day	118
Mardi Gras	Shrove Tuesday	125
Joyeuses Pâques	Happy Easter	133
Halloween	Halloween	141

Introduction

This book was written by a secondary and a primary school teacher to provide key vocabulary for twenty topics, and to give teachers ideas for introducing, teaching, reinforcing and extending new vocabulary. Each topic has key vocabulary, word matching cards, an activity sheet, a puzzle page, and ideas for extending learning through sentence building. Many topics also have picture cards. Using the book can support the teacher in covering many of the objectives in the **Framework for Modern Foreign Languages** using a choice of fun and lively activities.

The key vocabulary pages can be enlarged to A3 for classroom display, or photocopied and laminated as reference cards. The word and picture matching cards can be used in many ways. Lessons should begin with work on the Oracy Objectives in the **Framework** by repeating the new words after the teacher and playing some flashcard games. The children can then work in mixed ability pairs, using the photocopiable sheets from the book. They can match the words face up, then progress to matching them face down in a 'pairs' game. They could also play snap. They could glue the English words on an A3 sheet and carefully write the French words next to them, or glue on the French words, and draw pictures to match each word, and progress to writing the new words from memory.

The sentence building sheets can further develop the children's language skills, reinforcing vocabulary by using it in simple sentences. The suggestions work towards the Literacy Objectives in the **Framework** and will further develop children's reading and writing skills. The puzzle pages reinforce the language further in a fun way, and could also be used for homework.

Children should be encouraged to think about how they learn new vocabulary, a skill the Language Learning Strategies section of the **Framework** encourages. **Visual learners** will benefit from the matching sheets, and from drawing pictures to match. **Auditory learners** will benefit from repeating after the teacher and hearing their partner say the new words, perhaps during a game of snap. **Kinaesthetic learners** will enjoy cutting the words up and matching them. Using a variety of methods will cater for the many different learning styles in a class and ensure that confidence and ability grow alongside each other.

The Knowledge about Language section of the **Framework** encourages children to focus on their pronunciation and intonation. It is crucial that the language on the sheets is modelled by the teacher, or using a CD or Internet resource, and followed up with songs and rhymes.

We use all of the resources in this book ourselves with much success. Our pupils enjoy the challenge of learning new vocabulary and complete the guided sheets with pride and confidence. We sincerely hope that you and your pupils enjoy learning and using their new vocabulary.

Les chiffres Key vocabulary

0	*zéro*
1	*un*
2	*deux*
3	*trois*
4	*quatre*
5	*cinq*
6	*six*
7	*sept*
8	*huit*
9	*neuf*
10	*dix*
11	*onze*
12	*douze*

Allez, on compte! We are going to count.

Les chiffres
✂ Matching cards

1	2	3
4	5	6
un	*deux*	*trois*
quatre	*cinq*	*six*

Les chiffres ✂ Matching cards

7	8	9
10	11	12
sept	huit	neuf
dix	onze	douze

Les chiffres

Activity sheet

Nom: .... Date: ....

I can name and recognize numbers from 1 to 12 in French.
Write the word for each number carefully and neatly in the grid below. Then draw the correct number of items to match. For example, write *un* and draw one object. It can be anything you like, maybe a smiley face.

un	six	huit	trois	douze	sept
....	....	....	....	....	....
deux	quatre	neuf	cinq	onze	dix
....	....	....	....	....	....

Extra!

What is the highest number that you know in French? Write it in words.

Les chiffres

Puzzle page

Cherche les mots dans la grille.
Search for the words in the grid.

zéro	q	g	c	o	d	o	u	z	e	h
un	s	u	a	j	m	l	n	e	u	f
deux	j	o	a	p	l	s	e	w	x	v
trois	s	e	p	t	o	m	g	d	f	c
quatre	i	o	u	x	r	z	u	i	l	i
cinq	x	j	t	o	d	e	u	x	p	n
six	h	g	r	w	r	b	v	b	c	q
sept	e	t	o	y	s	o	n	z	e	d
huit	h	u	i	t	r	q	p	o	y	t
neuf	p	o	s	w	z	é	r	o	o	m

zéro, un, deux, trois, quatre, cinq, six, sept, huit, neuf, dix, onze, douze

Remets les lettres dans l'ordre.
Put the letters in order.

nu	un
ptes	....
uqtaer	....
roits	....
uiht	....
qinc	....
xdeu	....
fenu	....
xsi	....
nzoe	....
xid	....
eduoz	....

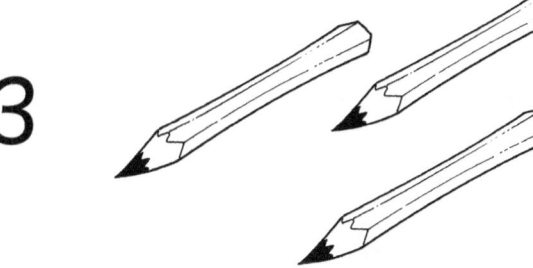

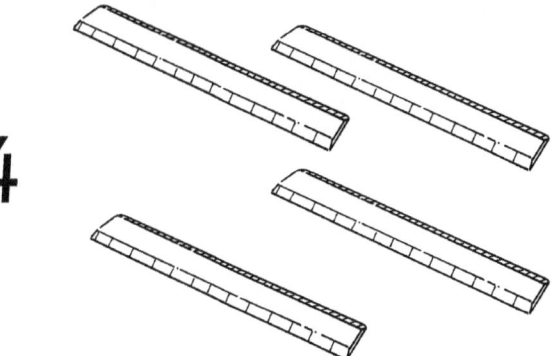

Les chiffres — Sentence building

Ask a question
Tu as quel âge?	How old are you?
J'ai dix ans.	I am ten years old.

Play a game
C'est quel numéro?	What number am I thinking of?
C'est le numéro sept?	Is it number seven?
Non, c'est plus.	No, higher.
Non, c'est moins.	No, lower.
Oui, bonne réponse.	Yes, good answer.

Count items in the room
Il y a combien d'enfants?	How many children are there?
Il y a combien de chaises?	How many chairs are there?
Il y a …	There are …

Sing a song
Use a song to reinforce vocabulary such as 'Comptons jusqu'à 20' from *J'aime Chanter!*

Les jours

Key vocabulary

lundi	Monday
mardi	Tuesday
mercredi	Wednesday
jeudi	Thursday
vendredi	Friday
samedi	Saturday
dimanche	Sunday

Quel jour sommes-nous?
What day is it?

Quelle est la date aujourd'hui?
What's today's date?

C'est lundi!
It's Monday!

Les jours

✂ **Matching cards**

lundi	Monday
mardi	Tuesday
mercredi	Wednesday
jeudi	Thursday
vendredi	Friday
samedi	Saturday
dimanche	Sunday

Les jours Activity sheet

Nom: .... Date: ....

I know the days of the week in French.
Write each day of the week carefully and then draw a picture to show what you may do on that day.

lundi	
mardi	
mercredi	
jeudi	
vendredi	
samedi	
dimanche	

Extra!

What do French children do on each day of the week?

Les jours

Puzzle page

Cherche les mots dans la grille.
Search for the words in the grid.

lundi
mardi
mercredi
jeudi
vendredi
samedi
dimanche
jour

v	n	u	o	j	o	u	r	u	r
b	e	g	f	e	e	o	p	e	s
d	n	n	h	i	d	u	o	u	i
i	m	b	d	n	s	a	d	e	w
m	e	r	c	r	e	d	i	i	l
a	l	m	n	b	e	g	h	s	l
n	h	s	a	m	e	d	i	j	u
c	k	x	c	m	z	a	i	p	n
h	o	l	y	u	r	e	w	s	d
e	p	o	o	t	m	a	r	d	i

Remets les lettres dans l'ordre.
Put the letters in order.

nudil	lundi
mrecrdei	....
drima	....
hemdianc	....
euijd	....
masedi	....
idrenved	....

Quel jour sommes-nous?
What day is it?

_ _ _ d _   lundi
_ _ _ _ r _ _ _
_ _ m _ _ _ _ _
_ e _ _ _
_ _ _ d _ _ _ _

Les jours — Sentence building

Ask a question

Quel jour sommes-nous? — What day is it?
C'est lundi/mardi. — It's Monday/Tuesday.

Quelle est la date aujourd'hui? — What is today's date?
C'est lundi 4 mai. — It's Monday the 4th of May.

Don't forget to use *premier* in French for 'the 1st'.
C'est le samedi premier mars. — It's Saturday 1st March.

Add a preference
Quel est ton jour préféré? — Which is your favourite day?

 *Je préfère le samedi.* — I like Saturday best.

 *Je déteste le lundi.* — I hate Mondays.

Sing a song
Use a song to reinforce vocabulary such as 'Les jours de la semaine' from *J'aime Chanter!*

Les mois

Key vocabulary

janvier	January
février	February
mars	March
avril	April
mai	May
juin	June
juillet	July
août	August
septembre	September
octobre	October
novembre	November
décembre	December

Quelle est la date de ton anniversaire?
When is your birthday?

Mon anniversaire, c'est le dix janvier.
My birthday is on the 10th of January.

Quelle est la date aujourd'hui?
What is today's date?

C'est lundi 23 juin.
It's Monday, the 23rd June.

Les mois — Matching cards

janvier	January
février	February
mars	March
avril	April
mai	May
juin	June

Les mois ✂ Matching cards

juillet	July
août	August
septembre	September
octobre	October
novembre	November
décembre	December

Les mois

Activity sheet

Nom: .... Date: ....

I know the months of the year in French.

Carefully write the months of the year in French. Draw a symbol for an event in each month. For example, a rabbit for Easter.

janvier

Extra!

Quelle est la date de ton anniversaire?

When is your birthday?

Les mois

Puzzle page

Cherche les mots dans la grille.
Search for the words in the grid.

janvier
février
mars
avril
mai
juin
juillet
août
septembre
octobre
novembre
décembre

a	o	m	a	r	s	a	m	v	a
j	a	n	v	i	e	r	a	r	v
u	u	b	r	t	p	s	i	n	r
i	t	i	y	u	t	w	n	o	i
l	b	v	n	v	e	s	z	v	l
l	a	x	c	r	m	t	e	e	a
e	o	c	t	o	b	r	e	m	n
t	û	u	i	o	r	v	x	b	l
s	t	d	é	c	e	m	b	r	e
a	e	g	f	é	v	r	i	e	r

Remets les lettres dans l'ordre.
Put the letters in order.

nraejvi   *janvier*
arms   ....
rbmedecé   ....
ima   ....
ejtlilu   ....
unji   ....
vrfréie   ....
ûota   ....
permebest   ....
teorocb   ....
iarlv   ....
ebnomerv   ....

C'est quel mois?
What month is it?

_ _ _ v _ _ _   *janvier*
_ _ r _
_ u _ _ _ _
_ _ _ t
_ _ _ e _ _ _ _

Les mois Sentence building

Ask a question
Quelle est la date de ton anniversaire? When is your birthday?
Mon anniversaire, c'est le dix janvier. My birthday is on the
 10th of January.

Add a preference
Quel est ton mois préféré? Which is your favourite month?

 *Je préfère le mois de mai.* My favourite is May.

 *Je déteste le mois de janvier.* I hate January.

Add the seasons
(au) printemps (in) spring
(en) été (in) summer
(en) automne (in) autumn
(en) hiver (in) winter

Janvier est en hiver. January is in winter.
Mai est au printemps. May is in spring.

Sing a song
Use a song to reinforce vocabulary such as 'Les mois l'anée' from *J'aime Chanter!*

Ma famille

Key vocabulary

mon père	my father
ma mère	my mother
mon beau-père	my step-dad
ma belle-mère	my step-mum
mon frère	my brother
ma soeur	my sister
mon grand-père	my grandad
ma grand-mère	my grandma
mon oncle	my uncle
ma tante	my aunt
mon cousin	my cousin (boy)
ma cousine	my cousin (girl)

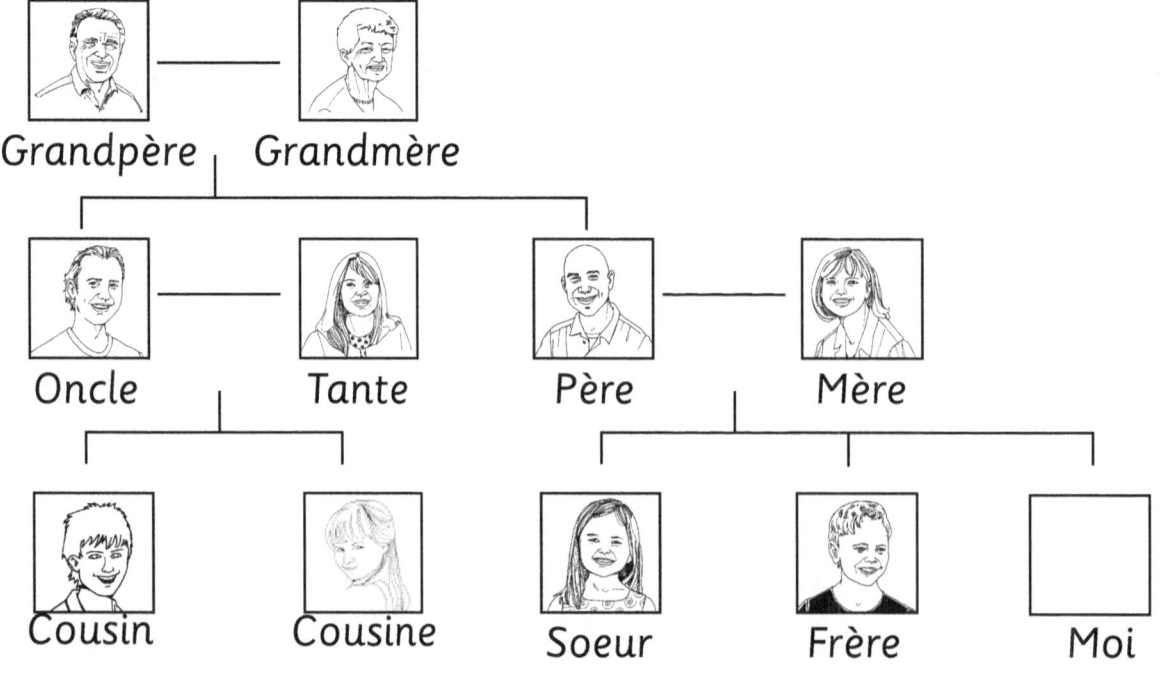

Grandpère   Grandmère

Oncle   Tante   Père   Mère

Cousin   Cousine   Soeur   Frère   Moi

Ma famille ✂ Matching cards

père	father
mère	mother
frère	brother
soeur	sister
grand-père	grandad
grand-mère	grandma
tante	aunt
oncle	uncle

Ma famille

✂ Picture cards

père	
mère	
frère	
soeur	
grand-père	
grand-mère	
tante	
oncle	

Ma famille

Activity sheet

Nom: .... Date: ....

I know the names of family members in French.

Draw yourself in the centre of this sheet and label it *Moi* (me). Then add your immediate family and label them. For example: *Ma soeur, Rebecca*.

Extra!

Il y a combien de personnes chez toi?

How many people live with you?

Ma famille

Puzzle page

Cherche les mots dans la grille.
Search for the words in the grid.

père
mère
beau-père
belle-mère
frère
soeur
grand-père
grand-mère
oncle
tante
cousin
cousine

```
c  o  u  s  i  n  e  b  u  r  s  s
o  g  m  h  o  t  a  n  t  e  g  o
u  l  r  o  u  s  a  o  n  c  l  e
s  r  t  a  n  m  p  l  o  m  w  u
i  g  r  a  n  d  p  è  r  e  w  r
n  p  o  d  r  d  e  a  w  d  c  v
m  b  e  l  l  e  m  è  r  e  l  k
m  è  r  e  f  d  v  è  b  n  i  o
j  b  b  e  a  u  p  è  r  e  n  m
p  è  r  e  l  f  r  è  r  e  s  z
```

Remets les lettres dans l'ordre.
Put the letters in order.

nom peèr	*mon père*
am mèerdgrna	....
omn rèfer	....
am mrèe	....
nom lonce	....
am antte	....
am esour	....
nom prndrgaeè	....

Qui est-ce que?
Who is it?

_ a / _ o _ _ r   ma soeur

_ _ _ / p _ _ _

m _ / _ _ a _ _-m _ _ _

_ a / _ è _ _

_ _ n / _ _ _ l _

Ma famille — Sentence building

Add, 'dans ma famille, il y a …'
Dans ma famille il y a mon père, ma mère, ma soeur et moi.
In my family there is my father, my mother, my sister and me.

Add a name
Mon père s'appelle George.	My father's name is George.
Ma mère s'appelle Mary.	My mother's name is Mary.

Add an age
Mon père a 30 ans.	My father is 30 years old.
Ma soeur a 6 ans.	My sister is 6 years old.

Add a simple description
Mon père est grand/de taille moyenne/petit.
My father is tall/medium height/small.
Ma mère est grande/de taille moyenne/petite.
My mother is tall/medium height/small.

Add a characteristic
Mon frère est marrant.	My brother is funny.
Ma soeur est bavarde.	My sister is a chatterbox.

More characteristics

English	Masculine	Feminine
nice	*sympa*	*sympa*
chatty	*bavard*	*bavarde*
annoying	*embêtant*	*embêtante*
kind	*gentil*	*gentille*
lazy	*paresseux*	*paresseuse*
funny	*marrant*	*marrante*

Sing a song
Reinforce vocabulary by using a song such as 'La famille Souris' from *Chantez Plus Fort*.

Les couleurs

Key vocabulary

rouge	red
bleu	blue
vert	green
jaune	yellow
orange	orange
marron	brown
violet	purple
rose	pink
noir	black
blanc	white
or	gold
argent	silver
gris	grey

Quelle est ta couleur préférée?
What is your favourite colour?
Ma couleur préférée est ...
My favourite colour is ...

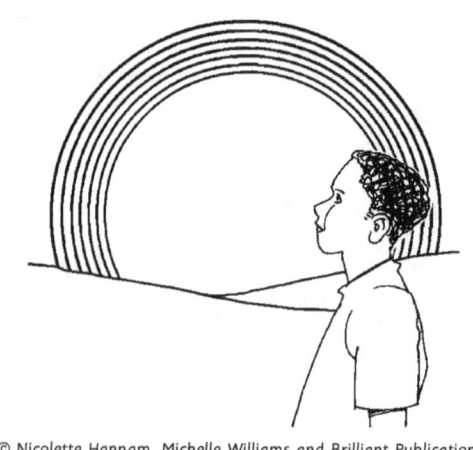

Les couleurs ✂ Matching cards

rouge	red
bleu	blue
orange	orange
jaune	yellow
vert	green
gris	grey

Les couleurs   ✂ Matching cards

rose	pink
violet	purple
noir	black
blanc	white
or	gold
argent	silver

Les couleurs

Matching cards

Coloriez les cartes!
Colour the cards!

rouge	
bleu	
orange	
jaune	
vert	
rose	

Les couleurs

✂ **Matching cards**

Coloriez les cartes!
Colour the cards!

violet	
noir	
blanc	
or	
argent	
gris	

Les couleurs — Activity sheet

Nom: .... Date: ....

I know the colours in French.
Use the vocabulary box below to help you to draw some shapes.
Then colour them the right colour.

un carré rouge	un cercle jaune	un rectangle bleu

un triangle vert	un diamant blanc	un rhombe noir

un carré marron	un cercle rose	un triangle violet

un carré	a square		un cercle	a circle
un rectangle	a rectangle		un triangle	a triangle
un diamant	a diamond		un rhombe	a rhombus

Les couleurs

Puzzle page

Cherche les mots dans la grille.
Search for the words in the grid.

rouge
bleu
vert
jaune
orange
marron
violet
rose
noir
blanc
or
argent
gris
couleur

n	i	o	o	w	v	i	o	l	e	t	g
p	o	r	a	n	g	e	q	w	s	r	r
r	r	i	y	o	p	m	l	w	d	j	i
o	r	r	r	s	a	c	e	i	b	a	s
s	t	r	e	e	d	o	x	v	m	u	k
e	l	v	e	r	t	u	b	l	a	n	c
b	l	e	u	t	m	l	n	b	r	e	d
w	t	r	o	u	g	e	r	y	r	m	n
a	s	t	e	r	i	u	c	s	o	m	p
t	o	e	d	w	a	r	g	e	n	t	x

Remets les lettres dans l'ordre.
Put the letters in order.

eougr   *rouge*
sroe   ....
uebl   ....
engora   ....

oinr   ....
clabn   ....
trev   ....
rorman   ....

C'est de quelle couleur?
What colour is it?

rouge + blanc =   rose
rouge + jaune = ...
bleu + jaune = ...
blanc + noir = ...
bleu + rouge = ...

Relie les mots et les images.
Match the words and pictures.

A   B   C

rouge   ....
vert   ....
bleu   ....

Les couleurs — Sentence building

Add a question and a preference

Quelle est ta couleur préférée?   What is your favourite colour?
Ma couleur préférée est le bleu.   My favourite colour is blue.

Add a noun

Remember colours in French follow the noun!

*J'ai un tee-shirt **noir.***   I have a black t-shirt.
*J'ai un sweat **vert.***   I have a green sweater.
*J'ai une robe **bleue.***   I have a blue dress.

**Don't forget to add an 'e' if the noun is feminine!
Look out for the irregular ones!
Use the table below to help you.**

Masculine	Feminine
vert	verte
bleu	bleue
brun	brune
gris	grise
noir	noire
rouge	rouge
jaune	jaune
blanc	blanche

Sing a song

Reinforce vocabulary by singing a song such as 'Les couleurs' from *Chantez Plus Fort*.

As-tu un animal?   Key vocabulary

un chien	a dog
un chat	a cat
un lapin	a rabbit
un hamster	a hamster
une souris	a mouse
un oiseau	a bird
un poisson	a fish
un cochon d'Inde	a guinea pig

As-tu un animal?
Do you have a pet?

Oui, j'ai un chien et un chat.
Yes, I've got a dog and a cat.

Je n'ai pas d'animal.
I haven't got any pets.

As-tu un animal? ✂ Matching cards

un chien	a dog
un chat	a cat
un lapin	a rabbit
un oiseau	a bird
un poisson	a fish
une souris	a mouse
un cochon d'Inde	a guinea pig
un hamster	a hamster

As-tu un animal? ✂ Picture cards

un chien	
un chat	
un lapin	
un oiseau	
un poisson	
un cochon d'Inde	
un hamster	

As-tu un animal?   Activity sheet

Nom: ....   Date: ....

I know the names of animals in French.
Draw the animals described below.
Make sure you use the right colour!

| un chien bleu | un chat vert | une souris rose |

| un oiseau blanc | un hamster rouge | un lapin jaune |

| un poisson violet | un cochon d'Inde noir |

Extra!

As-tu an animal?
Do you have a pet?

As-tu un animal? Puzzle page

Cherche les mots dans la grille.
Search for the words in the grid.

animal
chien
chat
lapin
hamster
souris
oiseau
poisson
cochon d'Inde

```
q s d v a n i m a l s d
h a m s t e r t u a o c
u i e w c z x t r p l h
p o r z u p i o n i b i
g c o c h o n d' i n d e
h o i p m i m a l s p n
c y s g l s y s j h g l
s h e o p s g p l o m j
j s a h s o u r i s o h
m o u t y n o s m a l s
```

Remets les lettres dans l'ordre.
Put the letters in order.

ctah   chat
palin   ....
rissou   ....
esahmtr   ....
soiuae   ....
nheic   ....
nossipo   ....

Devine l'animal.
Guess the animal.

u _ / l _ _ _ _
u _ _ / _ o u _ _ s
_ _ / _ _ _ t
_ _ / _ _ i _ _
_ _ / _ a _ _ _ _ _

Devine qui?
Who am I?

I bark. ....
I squeak. ....
I miaow. ....
I like carrots. ....

Relie les mots et les images.
Match the words to the pictures.

A   B   C

un chat   ....
un lapin   ....
un chien   ....

As-tu un animal? Sentence building

Ask a question
As-tu un animal?   Do you have a pet?

Use 'J'ai ...' or 'Je n'ai pas de ...'
Oui, j'ai un chat/un chien.   Yes, I have a cat/a dog.
Non, je n'ai pas d'animal.   No, I don't have a pet.

Add the connective 'et'
*J'ai un chien **et** un chat.*   I have a dog and a cat.

Add a name
J'ai un chat, 'Fluff.'   I have a cat, 'Fluff'.
*J'ai un chien **qui s'appelle** 'Patch'.*   I have dog called 'Patch'.

Add a colour
Remember colours in French follow the noun!
*J'ai un chat **gris**.*   I have a grey cat.
*J'ai un chien **brun**.*   I have a brown dog.
*J'ai une souris **grise**.*   I have a grey mouse.

Don't forget to add an 'e' if the noun is feminine!
Look out for the irregular ones!
Use the table (right) to help you.

Masculine	Feminine
vert	verte
bleu	bleue
brun	brune
gris	grise
noir	noire
rouge	rouge
jaune	jaune
blanc	blanche

Add an opinion
*J'aime **mon** chien/**ma** souris/**mes** poissons.*
I love my dog/my mouse/my fish.

*J'adore **mon** lapin/**ma** souris/**mes** chats.*
I adore my rabbit/my mouse/my cats.

Sing a song
Use a song such as 'Footfoot, tu as un animal' from *Chantez Plus Fort!*

La salle de classe — Key vocabulary

une porte	a door
une fenêtre	a window
une table	a table
une chaise	a chair
un ordinateur	a computer
un tableau	a board
un professeur	a teacher
un cahier	an exercise book
un livre	a text book
une trousse	a pencil case
une règle	a ruler
une gomme	an eraser
un crayon	a pencil
un taille-crayon	a pencil sharpener
un stylo	a pen
des ciseaux	scissors
des feutres	felt tips

Dans la salle de classe, il y a …
In the classroom, there is …

La salle de classe  Matching cards

une table	a table
une chaise	a chair
un livre	a book
un crayon	a pencil
un stylo	a pen
une règle	a ruler

La salle de classe — Matching cards

une gomme	an eraser
des feutres	felt tips
une porte	a door
une trousse	a pencil case
une fenêtre	a window
des ciseaux	scissors

La salle de classe ✂ Picture cards

une table	
une chaise	
un livre	
un crayon	
un stylo	
une règle	

La salle de classe — Picture cards

une gomme	
des feutres	
une porte	
une trousse	
une fenêtre	
des ciseaux	

© Nicolette Hannam, Michelle Williams and Brilliant Publications. Bonne idée

La salle de classe — Activity sheet

Nom: .... Date: ....

I know the names of objects in the classroom in French.

Unscramble these words and write them correctly. Then draw a picture to match each word.

une glerè	une fêerten	une trope
....	....	....

une ssoutre	une belta	un onyrac
....	....	....

une aieshc	des seicxua	une egmom
....	....	....

Extra!

Now choose two words to scramble yourself. Write them here.

La salle de classe — Puzzle page

Cherche les mots dans la grille.
Search for the words in the grid.

porte
fenêtre
table
chaise
tableau
professeur
cahier
livre
règle
gomme
crayon
stylo

```
f  e  n  ê  t  r  e  x  c  a
r  g  e  t  a  b  l  e  r  c
p  o  r  t  e  n  b  l  a  a
o  m  i  d  a  h  b  i  y  h
l  m  r  e  a  b  o  v  o  i
o  e  i  p  u  s  l  r  n  e
p  r  o  f  e  s  s  e  u  r
g  f  r  è  g  l  e  n  a  b
c  h  a  i  s  e  j  k  p  u
r  e  s  d  s  t  y  l  o  x
```

Remets les lettres dans l'ordre.
Put the letters in order.

letba — table
vreli — ....
ylost — ....
trope — ....
mmoge — ....
haices — ....
ryacno — ....

Devine?
What am I?

You write with me. ....
You write in me. ....
You sit on me. ....
I am different colours. ....
I am sharp. ....

Qu'est-ce que c'est?
What is it?

_ _ / _ _ y _ _
u _ _ / _ _ _ _ e
_ n / l _ _ _ _
_ _ _ / _ è _ _ _
u _ _ / _ _ _ _ s _

Relie les mots et les images.
Match the words to the pictures.

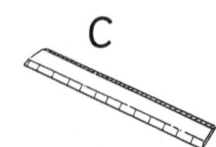

A   B   C

un règle — ....
un crayon — ....
des ciseaux — ....

La salle de classe Sentence building

Ask questions
Qu'est-ce qu'il y a dans la salle de classe?   What have you got in your classroom?

Qu'est-ce qu'il y a dans ton sac?   What have you got in your bag?

Use, 'dans la salle de classe, il y a …'
Dans la salle de classe, il y a une porte, un ordinateur …
In the classroom there is a door, a computer …
or
Dans mon sac, il y a un cahier, une gomme et un stylo.
In my bag, there is an exercise book, an eraser and a pen.

Reinforce numbers
Il y a combien de portes dans la salle de classe?
How many doors are there in the classroom?

Sing a song
Use a song such as 'La chanson des listes' from *Chantez Plus Fort!*

Au collège

Key vocabulary

l'anglais	English
le français	French
les maths	maths
les sciences	science
l'histoire	history
la géographie	geography
le sport	PE
le dessin	art
la musique	music
la technologie	design technology

Quelle est ta matière préférée?
What is your favourite subject?

J'aime ...	I like ...
J'adore ...	I love ...
Je n'aime pas ...	I don't like ...
Je déteste ...	I hate ...

Au collège  Matching cards

le français	French
l'anglais	English
les sciences	science
les maths	maths
l'histoire	history
la géographie	geography

Au collège — ✂ Matching cards

le sport	**PE**
le dessin	**art**
la technologie	**design technology**
la musique	**music**
j'aime ...	**I like ...**
je n'aime pas ...	**I don't like ...**

Au collège

Activity sheet

Nom: .... Date: ....

I know the names of school subjects in French.

Write each of the school subjects from the vocabulary box below in the correct column in the table to show how much you like each one.

J'adore ...	J'aime ...	Je n'aime pas ...	Je déteste ...

l'anglais	English	*le français*	French
les maths	maths	*les sciences*	science
l'histoire	history	*la géographie*	geography
le sport	PE	*le dessin*	art
la musique	music	*la technologie*	design technology

Extra!

Quelle est ta matière préférée?

Which is your favourite subject?

Au collège

Puzzle page

Cherche les mots dans la grille.
Search for the words in the grid.

anglais
français
maths
sciences
histoire
géographie
sport
dessin
musique

```
m  a  h  o  d  u  w  e  t  r
u  n  f  i  e  r  s  o  h  s
s  g  o  i  s  t  s  p  a  c
i  l  s  e  s  t  p  o  t  i
q  a  w  r  i  n  o  f  t  e
u  i  n  s  n  l  r  i  k  n
e  s  s  e  n  t  t  i  r  c
g  é  o  g  r  a  p  h  i  e
o  r  s  d  c  m  a  t  h  s
f  r  a  n  ç  a  i  s  l  m
```

Remets les lettres dans l'ordre.
Put the letters in order.

nilasga	*anglais*
ecsneics	....
psrto	....
snedis	....
quiemsu	....
asifnarç	....
esihrtio	....

Devine?
Which subject?

Times tables	Maths
Bonjour!	....
Bang the drum	....
Paints	....
Throw a ball	....

Relie les mots et les images.
Match the words and pictures.

A  B  C

La géographie ....
Le sport ....
Les maths ....

Au collège — Sentence building

Add a preference
Quelle est ta matière préférée? — What is your favourite subject?
Ma matière préférée est le français. — My favourite subject is French.

Add an opinion

 *J'aime le français.* — I like French.

 *J'adore le sport.* — I adore sport.

 Je n'aime pas le dessin. — I don't like art.

 *Je déteste la géographie.* — I hate geography.

Extend the opinion
C'est intéressant. — It's interesting.
C'est facile. — It's easy.
C'est ennuyeux. — It's boring.
C'est difficile. — It's difficult.

Sing a song
Reinforce vocabulary using a song such as 'Je me presente' in *Chantez Plus Fort!*

Bon appétit

Key vocabulary

une pizza	a pizza
un hot-dog	a hot-dog
un hamburger	a hamburger
une omelette	an omelette
des frites	chips
du poulet	chicken
du fromage	cheese
des légumes	vegetables
un sandwich	a sandwich
un gâteau	a cake
une glace	an ice-cream
des bonbons	sweets
un jus d'orange	an orange juice
un coca	a cola
une limonade	a lemonade
un café	a coffee
un thé	a tea
Je voudrais …	I would like …
s'il vous plaît	please
merci	thank you

Bon appétit

✂ Matching cards

une pizza	a pizza
des frites	chips
du poulet	chicken
des légumes	vegetables
du fromage	cheese
un gâteau	a cake

Bon appétit ✂ Matching cards

un thé	a tea
un coca	a cola
un café	a coffee
des bonbons	sweets
une glace	an ice-cream
Je voudrais …	I would like …

Bon appétit ✂ Picture cards

une pizza	
des frites	
du poulet	
des légumes	
du fromage	
un gâteau	

Bon appétit

✂ Picture cards

un thé	
un coca	
un café	
des bonbons	
une glace	
un hamburger	

Bon appétit — Activity sheet

Nom: .... Date: ....

I know the names of some food and drinks in French.
Draw and label a meal below, including a main dish, a dessert and a drink. Choose from the vocabulary in the box below.

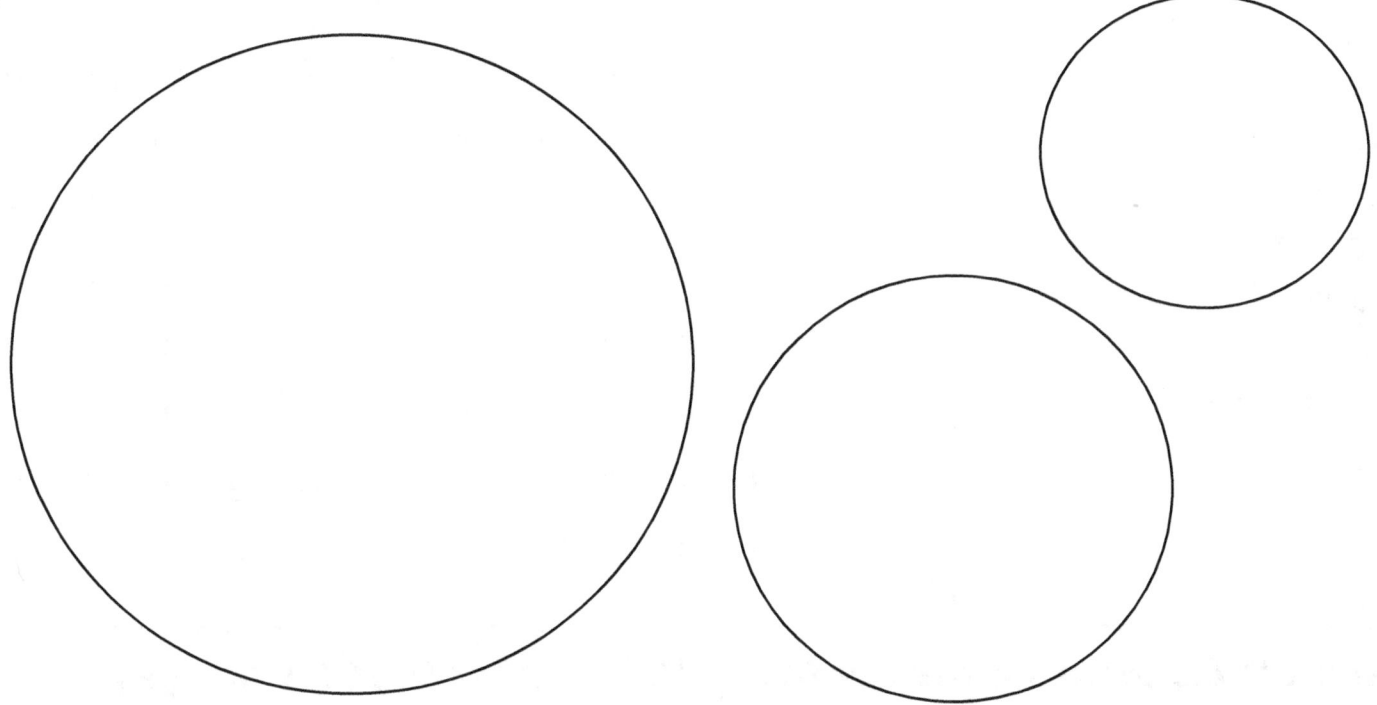

une pizza	a pizza	*un hot-dog*	a hot-dog
un hamburger	a hamburger	*une omelette*	an omelette
des frites	chips	*du poulet*	chicken
du fromage	cheese	*des légumes*	vegetables
un sandwich	a sandwich	*un gâteau*	a cake
une glace	an ice-cream	*des bonbons*	sweets
un jus d'orange	an orange juice	*un coca*	a cola
une limonade	a lemonade	*un café*	a coffee
un thé	a tea		

Extra!

Qu'est-ce que tu aimes manger?
What do you like to eat?

Bon appétit

Puzzle page

Cherche les mots dans la grille.
Search for the words in the grid.

| hamburger |
| omelette |
| frites |
| poulet |
| fromage |
| légumes |
| gâteau |
| glace |
| bonbons |
| jus d'orange |
| thé |

```
m  o  o  c  r  e  e  d  f  o  i  j
h  a  m  b  u  r  g  e  r  f  y  m
m  o  b  e  y  e  r  â  i  m  o  p
e  p  o  u  l  e  t  s  t  h  é  l
r  a  n  d  u  e  f  r  e  e  l  é
c  o  b  b  e  r  t  o  s  j  a  g
i  l  o  m  i  o  s  t  r  a  m  u
l  o  n  i  g  l  a  c  e  r  t  m
j  u  s  d'  o  r  a  n  g  e  r  e
a  d  d  f  r  o  m  a  g  e  l  s
```

Remets les lettres dans l'ordre.
Put the letters in order.

zizap	pizza
trifes	....
lagec	....
mforgea	....
teloup	....
écaf	....
snobbno	....

Relie les mots et les images.
Match the words to the pictures.

A  B  C

le poulet   ....
la pizza   ....
un coca   ....

Complète la liste.
Complete the list.

Snacks salés (savoury snacks)	Snacks sucrés (sweet snacks)	Boissons (drinks)
des frites	**gâteau**	**café**

Bon appétit — Sentence building

Make up a café dialogue
Useful vocabulary

A **Bonjour, Monsieur/Madame.**
Hello, Sir/Madam.
Vous désirez?
What would you like?

B **Je voudrais une pizza et des frites s'il vous plaît.**
I'd like a pizza and chips please.

A **Et avec ça?**
Anything else?

B **Je voudrais un jus d'orange s'il vous plaît.**
An orange juice please.
C'est délicieux.
It's delicious.
L'addition s'il vous plaît.
The bill please.

A **Voilà, 8 euros. Merci.**
Here you are, that's 8 euros. Thank you.

B **Merci. Au revoir.**
Thank you. Goodbye.

Add an opinion

 *J'aime le poulet.* — I like chicken.

 *J'adore les bonbons.* — I love sweets.

 *Je n'aime pas les légumes.* — I don't like vegetables.

 *Je déteste le fromage.* — I hate cheese.

Sing a song
Use a song such as 'Miam, miam, c'est délicieux' from *Chantez Plus Fort!*

Quel temps fait-il?

Key vocabulary

il pleut	it's raining
il neige	it's snowing
il fait du soleil	it's sunny
il fait du vent	it's windy
il fait du brouillard	it's foggy
il fait de l'orage	it's stormy
il fait froid	it's cold
il fait chaud	it's hot

aujourd'hui	today
demain	tomorrow

à Paris	in Paris
à Leeds	in Leeds
dans le nord	in the North
dans le sud	in the South
à l'est	in the East
à l'ouest	in the West

Quel temps fait-il? ✂ Matching cards

il pleut	it's raining
il neige	it's snowing
il fait froid	it's cold
il fait chaud	it's hot
il fait du vent	it's windy
il fait du soleil	it's sunny
il fait de l'orage	it's stormy
il fait du brouillard	it's foggy

Quel temps fait-il? ✂ Picture cards

il pleut	
il neige	
il fait froid	
il fait chaud	
il fait du vent	
il fait du soleil	
il fait de l'orage	
il fait du brouillard	

Quel temps fait-il? Activity sheet

Nom: .... Date: ....

I can describe the weather in French.

Draw lines to match each English weather phrase to the correct French phrase. Then draw a picture to match each French phrase.

It is stormy	*Il pleut*	
It is windy	*Il neige*	
It is raining	*Il fait du soleil*	
It is sunny	*Il fait du vent*	
It is snowing	*Il fait de l'orage*	

Extra!

Quel temps fait-il aujourd'hui?

What's the weather like today?

Quel temps fait-il? Puzzle page

Cherche les mots dans la grille.
Search for the words in the grid.

pleut
neige
soleil
vent
brouillard
orage
froid
chaud
demain
nord
sud
est
ouest

l	o	u	e	s	t	p	r	e	s
k	s	o	l	e	i	l	m	o	i
d	u	e	r	s	v	e	n	t	a
f	d	o	p	a	r	u	w	q	u
r	o	y	a	z	g	t	o	l	k
o	r	n	e	i	g	e	v	e	c
i	v	o	r	t	g	j	s	s	h
d	e	r	m	i	f	g	o	t	a
w	i	d	e	m	a	i	n	n	u
b	r	o	u	i	l	l	a	r	d

Remets les lettres dans l'ordre.
Put the letters in order.

li tleup — *il pleut*
li enieg — ....
li tfai duach — ....
li fita ud tvne — ....
li ftia drfio — ....
li iaft ud lsolie — ....

Relie les mots et les images.
Match the words and pictures.

A B C

Il neige. ....
Il pleut. ....
Il fait du soleil. ....

Quel temps fait-il? Sentence building

Add a town
À Mirfield, il fait chaud.	In Mirfield it's hot.
À Leeds, il pleut.	In Leeds it's raining.

Add a country
En France, il fait du soleil.	In France it's sunny.
En Angleterre, il fait du vent.	In England it's windy.

Use a weather map and make a forecast
Au nord, il neige.	In the North, it's snowing.
Au sud, il fait du brouillard.	In the South, it's foggy.
À l'est, il fait froid.	In the East, it's cold.
À l'ouest, il fait de l'orage.	In the West, it's stormy.

Add the seasons
Au printemps, il fait beau.	In the spring, it's nice weather.
En été, …	In the summer, …
En automne, …	In the autumn, …
En hiver, …	In the winter, …

Sing a song
Reinforce vocabulary by singing a song such as 'La chanson des listes' from *Chantez Plus Fort!*

Le corps

Key vocabulary

le visage	face
le nez	nose
la tête	head
la bouche	mouth
les yeux	eyes
les oreilles	ears
les cheveux	hair
les épaules	shoulders
le bras	arm
la main	hand
le ventre	stomach
le dos	back
la jambe	leg
le genou	knee
le pied	foot

J'ai mal à la tête.   I've got a headache.
J'ai mal au dos.   I've got backache.
J'ai mal aux oreilles.   I've got earache.

Le corps ✂ Matching cards

les yeux	eyes
la tête	head
les oreilles	ears
la bouche	mouth
la main	hand
la jambe	leg

Le corps ✂ Matching cards

le bras	arm
le ventre	tummy
le dos	back
le genou	knee
le pied	foot
les cheveux	hair

Le corps

✂ Picture cards

les yeux	
le visage	
les oreilles	
la bouche	
la main	
la jambe	

Le corps ✂ Picture cards

le bras	
le ventre	
le dos	
le genou	
le pied	
les cheveux	

Le corps

Activity sheet

Nom: .... Date: ....

I know the parts of the body in French.
Draw the monster that is described in the box below and colour it in.

> *Mon monstre a deux têtes,*
> *quatre bras et huit oreilles.*
> *Mon monstre a quatre mains,*
> *trois jambes et trois pieds.*
> *Mon monstre a une bouche,*
> *sept yeux et trois nez.*

Extra!

Which colours have you used on your monster? Can you list them, in French?

© Nicolette Hannam, Michelle Williams and Brilliant Publications. Bonne Idée.

Le corps — Puzzle page

Cherche les mots dans la grille.
Search for the words in the grid.

visage
nez
tête
bouche
yeux
oreilles
cheveux
épaules
main
dos
pied
jambe

```
j  t  r  e  o  i  c  n  e  z  e  s
a  r  b  e  q  r  z  i  o  n  b  t
m  s  é  d  f  g  e  l  k  d  o  s
b  u  p  r  e  r  h  i  m  p  u  o
e  m  a  i  n  l  y  k  l  d  c  f
o  i  u  s  p  i  e  d  x  l  h  c
v  r  l  a  s  h  u  p  k  l  e  m
c  h  e  v  e  u  x  o  p  h  l  s
o  p  s  h  j  r  t  t  ê  t  e  w
t  r  e  e  n  z  v  i  s  a  g  e
```

Remets les lettres dans l'ordre.
Put the letters in order.

al êett   la tête
al naim   ....
el srab   ....
el sdo   ....
al ubohce   ....
sel xyeu   ....
al ajmbe   ....

Ecris les légendes.
Write labels.

La tête

Le corps — Sentence building

Play a game using *'touchez ...'*
Touchez votre nez.　　Touch your nose.
Touchez vos yeux.　　Touch your eyes.

Reinforce numbers using *'j'ai'* for 'I have'
J'ai deux jambes.　　I have two legs.
J'ai une bouche.　　I have one mouth.

Introduce negatives
Je n'ai pas quatre genoux.　　I don't have four knees.

Introduce illness
J'ai mal à la tête.　　I have a headache.
J'ai mal au dos.　　I have backache.
J'ai mal aux oreilles.　　I have earache.

Add a song
Sing 'Head, shoulders, knees and toes' in French (literally in French you sing 'Head, shoulders, knees and feet'):

La tête, les épaules, les genoux et les pieds.
La tête, les épaules, les genoux et les pieds.

Les yeux, les oreilles, la bouche et le nez,
La tête, les épaules, les genoux et les pieds.

Mes passe-temps   Key vocabulary

Je joue au foot	I play football
Je joue au rugby	I play rugby
Je joue au tennis	I play tennis
Je fais du skate	I skateboard
Je fais du vélo	I ride my bike
Je fais du shopping	I go shopping
Je fais de l'équitation	I horse ride
Je fais de la natation	I swim
Je fais de la danse	I dance
J'écoute de la musique	I listen to music
Je regarde la télé	I watch TV
Je vais au cinéma	I go to the cinema
avec mes copains	with my friends
le week-end	at the weekend

Mes passe-temps ✂ Matching cards

Je joue au foot	I play football
Je fais du vélo	I ride my bike
Je fais de la natation	I swim
Je fais du shopping	I go shopping
Je vais au cinéma	I go to the cinema
Je regarde la télé	I watch TV

Mes passe-temps ✂ Matching cards

J'écoute de la musique	I listen to music
Je fais de la danse	I go dancing
Je joue au tennis	I play tennis
Je joue à l'ordinateur	I play on my computer
le week-end	at the weekend
avec mes copains	with my friends

Mes passe-temps ✂ Picture cards

Je joue au foot	
Je fais du vélo	
Je fais de la natation	
Je fais du shopping	
Je vais au cinéma	
Je regarde la télé	

Mes passe-temps ✂ Picture cards

J'écoute de la musique	
Je fais de la danse	
Je joue au tennis	
Je joue au rugby	
Je fais du skate	
Je fais de l'équitation	

Mes passe-temps

Activity sheet

Nom: .... Date: ....

I can describe my hobbies in French.

Draw yourself below. Then choose at least four phrases from the vocabulary box to describe your hobbies. Write them neatly around your picture. Illustrate your ideas.

Je joue au foot	I play football	*Je joue au rugby*	I play rugby
Je joue au tennis	I play tennis	*Je fais du skate*	I skateboard
Je fais du vélo	I ride my bike	*Je fais du shopping*	I shop
Je fais de l'équitation	I horse ride	*Je fais de la natation*	I swim
Je fais de la danse	I dance	*J'écoute de la musique*	I listen to music
Je regarde la télé	I watch TV		

Extra!

Quels sont tes passe-temps préférés?

What are your favourite hobbies?

Mes passe-temps

Puzzle page

Cherche les mots dans la grille.
Search for the words in the grid.

foot
rugby
tennis
skate
vélo
natation
danse
musique
cinéma
copains
week-end

d	r	e	c	o	p	a	i	n	s
a	r	t	i	x	t	e	r	g	k
n	o	h	n	a	e	r	e	b	a
s	a	y	é	r	n	f	o	o	t
e	r	t	m	o	n	h	g	k	e
o	r	s	a	m	i	v	é	l	o
p	u	r	e	t	s	y	u	n	p
o	g	m	u	s	i	q	u	e	m
i	b	r	e	a	s	o	y	t	g
m	y	w	e	e	k	e	n	d	n

Remets les lettres dans l'ordre.
Put the letters in order.

el toof   *le foot*
al sdaen   ....
el ménica   ....
ej ojue   ....
el nsntei   ....
al éétl   ....

Relie les mots et les images.
Match the words and pictures.

A   B   C

Je joue au tennis. ....
Je regarde la télé. ....
Je fais du vélo. ....

84

Mes passe-temps — Sentence building

Say when
Je joue au foot le week-end.   I play football at the weekend.
Je vais au cinéma le samedi.   I go to the cinema on Saturdays.

Say who with
Je joue au foot avec mon copain.   I play with my friend (boy).
Je joue au tennis avec ma copine.   I play tennis with my friend (girl).
Je fais du skate avec mes copains.   I skateboard with my friends.
Je vais au cinéma avec ma famille.   I go to the cinema with my family.

Add an opinion

 *J'aime le foot.*   I like football.

 *J'adore la danse.*   I love dancing.

 Je n'aime pas le rugby.   I don't like rugby.

 *Je déteste le tennis.*   I hate tennis.

Extend the opinion
C'est super.   It's great.
C'est génial.   It's brilliant.
C'est ennuyeux.   It's boring.

Les vêtements — Key vocabulary

une jupe	a skirt
une veste	a jacket
une robe	a dress
un tee-shirt	a t-shirt
un sweat	a sweatshirt
un jean	jeans
un pantalon	trousers
un short	shorts
un pull	a jumper
un pyjama	pyjamas
des baskets	trainers
des chaussures	shoes

Qu'est-ce que tu portes?
What are you wearing?

Je porte ... I am wearing ...

un jean bleu blue jeans
une robe bleue a blue dress

Les vêtements ✂ Matching cards

Je porte ...	I am wearing ...
un jean	jeans
un pantalon	trousers
un pull	a jumper
un tee-shirt	a t-shirt
un short	shorts

Les vêtements ✂ Matching cards

un pyjama	pyjamas
une robe	a dress
une veste	a jacket
une jupe	a skirt
des baskets	trainers
des chaussures	shoes

Les vêtements ✂ Picture cards

Je porte …	
un jean	
un pantalon	
un pull	
un tee-shirt	
un short	

Les vêtements

✂ Picture cards

un pyjama	
une robe	
une veste	
une jupe	
des baskets	
des chaussures	

Les vêtements   Activity sheet

Nom: .... Date: ....

I can name items of clothing in French.
Draw and colour the clothing described here.

une robe bleue

un pantalon vert

des baskets noires et jaunes

un pull rouge

Extra!

Now draw and describe some of your clothes, in French.

Les vêtements

Puzzle page

Cherche les mots dans la grille.
Search for the words in the grid.

jupe
veste
robe
tee-shirt
sweat
jean
pantalon
short
pull
pyjama
baskets
chaussures

```
j u m e t r p u l l
s o p y j a m a n t
c h a u s s u r e s
s u n t y o p v e w
t r t o j u p e m e
s b a s k e t s u a
h o l i d v y t j t
o r o b e r y e e t
r u n b t e r n a b
t e e s h i r t n x
```

Remets les lettres dans l'ordre.
Put the letters in order.

nu neaj   un jean
nu lulp   ....
nue puje   ....
enu esvte   ....
sed skabest   ....
nu trosh   ....

Relie les mots et les images.
Match the words and pictures.

A   B   C

une jupe   ....
des baskets   ....
un jean   ....

Qu'est-ce que c'est?
What is it?

_ n / _ _ _ t _ _ _ n
_ _ e / _ _ b _
d _ _ / _ _ _ _ s s _ _ _ _
_ _ / _ y _ _ _ _

92

© Nicolette Hannam, Michelle Williams and Brilliant Publications. Bonne Idée.

Les vêtements

Sentence building

Describe what you are wearing

Qu'est-ce que tu portes? — What are you wearing?
Je porte un jean et un tee-shirt. — I'm wearing jeans and a t-shirt.

Describe your ideal uniform

Mon uniforme idéal, c'est un pull et un jean.
My ideal uniform is a jumper and jeans.

Add a colour
Remember colours in French follow the noun!

J'ai un tee-shirt noir. — I have a black t-shirt.
J'ai un un sweat vert. — I have a green sweatshirt.
Je porte une robe bleue. — I'm wearing a blue dress.

Don't forget to add an 'e' if the noun is feminine!
Look out for the irregular ones!
Use the table below to help you.

Masculine	Feminine
vert	verte
bleu	bleue
brun	brune
gris	grise
noir	noire
rouge	rouge
jaune	jaune
blanc	blanche

En ville

Key vocabulary

la boulangerie	the bakery
la pâtisserie	the cake shop
la poste	the post office
la piscine	the swimming pool
la plage	the beach
la gare	the station
l'école	the school
le supermarché	the supermarket
le marché	the market
le café	the café
le cinéma	the cinema
le centre sportif	the leisure centre
le musée	the museum
l'hôtel de ville	the town hall
Voici le cinéma.	Here is the cinema.
Où habites-tu?	Where do you live?
J'habite à Leeds.	I live in Leeds.
Dans ma ville, il y a …	In my town, there is …

En ville ✂ Matching cards

la boulangerie	the bakery
la pâtisserie	the cake shop
la gare	the train station
la poste	the post office
le musée	the museum
le supermarché	the supermarket

En ville ✂ Matching cards

le café	the café
la piscine	the swimming pool
l'école	the school
le cinéma	the cinema
la plage	the beach
la ville	the town

En ville

✂ Picture cards

la boulangerie	
la pâtisserie	
la gare	
la poste	
le musée	
le supermarché	

© Nicolette Hannam, Michelle Williams and Brilliant Publications. Bonne Idée.

En ville

✂ Picture cards

le café	
la piscine	
l'école	
le cinéma	
la plage	
la ville	

En ville

Activity sheet

Nom: .... Date: ....

I can name places in a town in French.

For each of the buildings below, draw items that can be bought or found inside it.

| la pâtisserie | le marché | l'école |

| la piscine | la poste | le café |

Extra!

Which currency is used in French shops?

99

© Nicolette Hannam, Michelle Williams and Brilliant Publications. Bonne Idée.

En ville

Puzzle page

Cherche les mots dans la grille.
Search for the words in the grid.

boulangerie
pâtisserie
poste
piscine
plage
gare
école
supermarché
marché
café
cinéma
musée

```
a  b  o  u  l  a  n  g  e  r  i  e
p  â  t  i  s  s  e  r  i  e  c  d
i  l  n  e  s  t  t  u  n  g  l  p
s  b  a  c  i  n  é  m  a  b  p  o
c  h  e  g  a  r  e  m  s  m  t  s
i  a  j  l  e  e  r  m  b  u  n  t
n  a  f  c  a  r  d  s  e  s  w  e
e  g  n  é  m  a  r  c  h  é  m  p
c  h  o  k  l  é  c  o  l  e  m  n
d  s  u  p  e  r  m  a  r  c  h  é
```

Remets les lettres dans l'ordre.
Put the letters in order.

eun eairbgnleou   *une boulangerie*
al aegr   ....
el féca   ....
al pnsicie   ....
el émcnai   ....
al pegla   ....

Qu'est-ce que c'est?
Where am I?

You can swim here.   *la piscine*
You can watch films here.   ....
You buy stamps here.   ....
You buy cakes here.   ....
You have lessons here.   ....

Relie les mots et les images.
Match the words and pictures.

A   B

C

une piscine   ....
un café   ....
un cinéma   ....

En ville — Sentence building

Say where you live using *'j'habite à ...'*
J'habite à Leeds.   I live in Leeds.

Say what there is in your town
Dans ma ville, **il y a** ...   In my town **there is** a ...

Use some prepositions
La banque est **en face de** la poste.
The bank is **opposite** the post office.

La pisicne est **à côté de** la gare.
The swimming pool is **next to** the station.

La boulangerie est **entre** la piscine et la banque.
The bakery is **between** the pool and the bank.

Le café est **devant** l'école.
The café is **in front** of the school.

Le supermarché est **derrière** la banque.
The supermarket is **behind** the bank.

Ma maison

Key vocabulary

la maison	the house
l'appartement	the flat
les pièces	the rooms
en haut	upstairs
en bas	downstairs
le salon	the lounge
la cuisine	the kitchen
la salle à manger	the dining room
la salle de bains	the bathroom
les waters	the toilet
la chambre	the bedroom
ma chambre	my bedroom
le garage	the garage
le jardin	the garden

Dans ma maison, il y a …   In my house, there is …

Ma maison ✂ Matching cards

la maison	the house
l'appartement	the flat
la cuisine	the kitchen
la salle à manger	the dining room
la salle de bains	the bathroom
le salon	the lounge

Ma maison

✂ Matching cards

la chambre	the bedroom
les waters	the toilet
le garage	the garage
le jardin	the garden
en haut	upstairs
en bas	downstairs

Ma maison

✂ Picture cards

la maison	
l'appartement	
la cuisine	
la salle à manger	
la salle de bains	
le salon	

Ma maison

✂ Picture cards

la chambre	
les waters	
le garage	
le jardin	
en haut	
en bas	

Ma maison

Activity sheet

Nom: .... Date: ....

I can name the rooms in a house in French.
Use the space below to draw and label a typical house, using the vocabulary in the box below. You may have to draw two separate floors.

en haut	upstairs	**en bas**	downstairs
le salon	the lounge	**la cuisine**	the kitchen
la salle à manger	the dining room	**les waters**	the toilet
la salle de bains	the bathroom	**la chambre**	the bedroom
ma chambre	my bedroom	**le garage**	the garage
le jardin	the garden		

Ideas for home: you could draw and label your dream house on large paper. Or build a 3D model.

Extra!

Can you name any types of furniture, in French? You could use a dictionary to help you.

Ma maison

Puzzle page

Cherche les mots dans la grille.
Search for the words in the grid.

maison
appartement
pièces
haut
bas
salon
cuisine
salle de bains
chambre
garage
jardin

```
w o l i v e r g m o i l
s a l l e d e b a i n s
a p t o j l e t i e s c
l i t e a h c o s t r u
o è y u r c h l o m p i
n c e g d s a x n o o s
m e n t i b m a w v h i
a s t i n g b a s h a n
v h l k g a r a g e u e
a p p a r t e m e n t z
```

Remets les lettres dans l'ordre.
Put the letters in order.

al asimon   la maison
al uicisne   ....
el rgagae   ....
el rijdan   ....
el lasno   ....
am hcamreb   ....

C'est quelle pièce?
Which room is it?

Where you sleep.   la chambre
Where you cook.   ....
Where you play outside. ....
Where you watch TV.   ....
Where you get washed.   ....

Relie les mots et les images.
Match the words and pictures.

A   B

C

le jardin   ....
ma chambre   ....
la salle de bains ....

108

Ma maison

Sentence building

Use 'dans ma maison, il y a ...'
Dans ma maison, il y a la cuisine, la salle de bains ...
In my house there is the kitchen, the bathroom ...

Use a simple description
Ma maison est grande/petite.	My house is large/small.
Ma chambre est grande/petite.	My bedroom is large/small.
Ma chambre est bleue.	My bedroom is blue.

Describe a fantasy house
Dans ma maison de rêves, il y a cinq salles de bains et dix chambres.
In my dream house there are five bathrooms and ten bedrooms.

Ask a question
As tu une pièce préférée?   Do you have a favourite room?

Joyeux Noël

Key vocabulary

Joyeux Noël	Happy Christmas
le père Noël	Father Christmas
la veille de Noël	Christmas Eve
un sapin	a Christmas tree
un bonhomme de neige	a snowman
un renne	a reindeer
un cadeau	a present
les lutins	the elves
une boule	a bauble
la dinde	turkey
l'étoile	the star
un ange	an angel
les rois mages	the Three Kings
les bergers	the shepherds
l'enfant Jésus	the baby Jesus
une étable	a stable
une crèche	a crib

Joyeux Noël ✂ Matching cards

Joyeux Noël	**Happy Christmas**
le père Noël	**Father Christmas**
un sapin	**a Christmas tree**
un bonhomme de neige	**a snowman**
un cadeau	**a present**
un renne	**a reindeer**

Joyeux Noël — Matching cards

un ange	an angel
les Rois Mages	the Three Kings
les bergers	the shepherds
une crèche	a crib
une boule	a bauble
les lutins	the elves

Joyeux Noël ✂ Picture cards

Joyeux Noël	Happy Christmas
le père Noël	
un sapin	
un bonhomme de neige	
un cadeau	
un renne	

Joyeux Noël

✂ Picture cards

un ange	
les Rois Mages	
les bergers	
une crèche	
une boule	
les lutins	

Joyeux Noël

Activity sheet

Nom: .... Date: ....

I know some Christmas words in French.

Draw lines to match up the English Christmas phrase to the correct French phrase. Then draw a picture to match each French phrase.

Father Christmas	*un bonhomme de neige*
a snowman	*les Rois Mages*
a Christmas tree	*un cadeau*
the Three Kings	*le père Noël*
a present	*un sapin*

Extra!

What colours does le père Noël wear? Can you list them in French?

115

Joyeux Noël — Puzzle page

Cherche les mots dans la grille.
Search for the words in the grid.

Joyeux Noël
père Noël
sapin
renne
cadeau
lutins
boule
dinde
étoile
ange
bergers
enfant Jésus
étable
crèche

```
j o y e u x n o ë l x é
g o c r è c h e h a t t
g r u p è r e n o ë l a
b e e c o s a p i n g b
e n f a n t j é s u s l
r n o d r u r t o l d e
g e n e r t s o o d i m
e g h a l u t i n s n o
r b o u l e r l u i d m
s c p j a n g e l k e n
```

Remets les lettres dans l'ordre.
Put the letters in order.

el rèep ëonl	*le père Noël*
nu adcaue	....
neu gean	....
nu pasin	....
esl gerbser	....
neu loube	....

Qu'est-ce que c'est?
What is it?

_ _ / s _ _ _ _   un sapin
_ _ / _ n _ _
_ n _ / _ _ è _ _ _
_ _ _ / b _ _ _ _

Relie les mots et les images.
Match the words and pictures.

A   B   C

le sapin ....
le père Noël ....
le bonhomme de neige ....

Joyeux Noël

Sentence building

Dessine une carte.
Make a Christmas or New Year card.

Joyeux Noël!	Happy Christmas
Bonne Année!	Happy New Year
Chère Maman	Dear Mum
Cher Papa	Dear Dad
Bisous	Love from

Use 'il y a …' to describe a nativity scene
Il y a un ange et l'étoile, les bergers …
There is an angel and the star, the shepherds …

Sing a song
Use 'Vive le Vent' from *Chantez Plus Fort!*

Saint-Valentin

Key vocabulary

Joyeuse Saint-Valentin	Happy Valentine's Day
Je t'aime	I love you
Veux-tu m'épouser	Will you marry me!
Sors avec moi!	Go out with me!
mon petit copain	my boyfriend
ma petite copine	my girlfriend
un bisou	a kiss
un coeur	a heart
un cadeau	a present
une carte	a card
des fleurs	flowers
des chocolats	chocolates
chéri/chérie	dear
Cupidon	Cupid

Saint-Valentin ✂ Matching cards

Saint-Valentin	**Valentine's Day**
Cupidon	**Cupid**
des chocolats	**chocolates**
des fleurs	**flowers**
Je t'aime	**I love you**
Veux-tu m'épouser?	**Will you marry me?**

Saint-Valentin ✂ Matching cards

un bisou	a kiss
un cadeau	a present
une carte	a card
mon petit copain	my boyfriend
ma petite copine	my girlfriend
Sors avec moi!	Go out with me!

Saint-Valentin ✂ Picture cards

Cupidon	
des chocolats	
des fleurs	
Je t'aime	
un bisou	
un cadeau	
une carte	
un coeur	

Saint-Valentin — Activity sheet

Nom: .... Date: ....

I know some Valentine's Day words in French.

Unscramble these words and write them correctly. Then draw a picture to match each word.

nu rceou

....

eun treac

....

nu dacaue

....

nu sbiou

....

esd lefusr

....

eds hocclatso

....

ndoCpiu

....

Extra!

Now choose two words to scramble yourself. Write them here.

Saint-Valentin

Puzzle page

Cherche les mots dans la grille.
Search for the words in the grid.

petit copain
petite copine
bisou
coeur
cadeau
carte
fleurs
chocolats
Cupidon
aime
épouser
chérie

```
é  m  c  h  o  c  o  l  a  t  s  x
p  l  u  a  p  l  o  n  g  a  m  p
o  r  p  i  d  r  a  k  l  i  n  c
u  p  i  r  g  e  f  x  n  m  l  h
s  u  d  r  o  c  a  r  t  e  b  é
e  x  o  n  f  l  e  u  r  s  t  r
r  i  n  g  h  k  v  c  l  o  t  i
p  e  t  i  t  e  c  o  p  i  n  e
c  o  e  u  r  m  x  b  i  s  o  u
p  e  t  i  t  c  o  p  a  i  n  q
```

Remets les lettres dans l'ordre.
Put the letters in order.

nodpuci   *Cupidon*
sed lfsuer   ....
nu adcuea   ....
nue trace   ....
nu soubi   ....
ej t'amie   ....

Qu'est-ce que c'est?
What is it?

s _ _ _ _ _ / v _ _ _ _ _ _ _ _
_ _ p _ _ _ _
_ _ s / f _ _ _ _ _
_ _ e / _ _ _ t _
m _ _ / _ e _ _ _ / c _ _ _ _ _

Saint-Valentin

Sentence building

Faites une carte de Saint-Valentin.
Make a Valentine's Day card.

Joyeuse Saint-Valentin	Happy Valentine's Day
Cher Paul	Dear Paul
Chère Julie	Dear Julie
Je t'aime	I love you
Bisous	Love from

Écris une lettre.
Write a letter.

Ma Chérie	Darling (girl)
Mon Chéri	Darling (boy)
Tu es belle	You (female) are beautiful
Tu es beau	You (male) are handsome
Je t'aime	I love you
Je t'embrasse	Kisses

Mardi gras

Key vocabulary

une crêpe	a pancake
un oeuf	an egg
le lait	milk
la farine	flour
le beurre	butter
du sel	salt
une poêle	a pan
un déguisement	a costume
une fête	a party
un masque	a mask
un défilé	a parade
un char	a float

Mardi gras — Matching cards

une crêpe	a pancake
le beurre	butter
la farine	flour
un oeuf	an egg
le lait	milk
une poêle	a pan

Mardi gras

✂ Matching cards

du sel	salt
un déguisement	a costume
un défilé	a parade
un char	a float
une fête	a party
un masque	a mask

Mardi gras

✂ Picture cards

une crêpe	
le beurre	
la farine	
un oeuf	
le lait	
une poêle	

Mardi gras

✂ Picture cards

du sel	
un déguisement	
un défilé	
un char	
une fête	
un masque	

Mardi gras — Activity sheet

Nom: .... Date: ....

I know some Shrove Tuesday words in French.
Draw and label the ingredients of a pancake in the bowl below. Use the vocabulary box to help you.

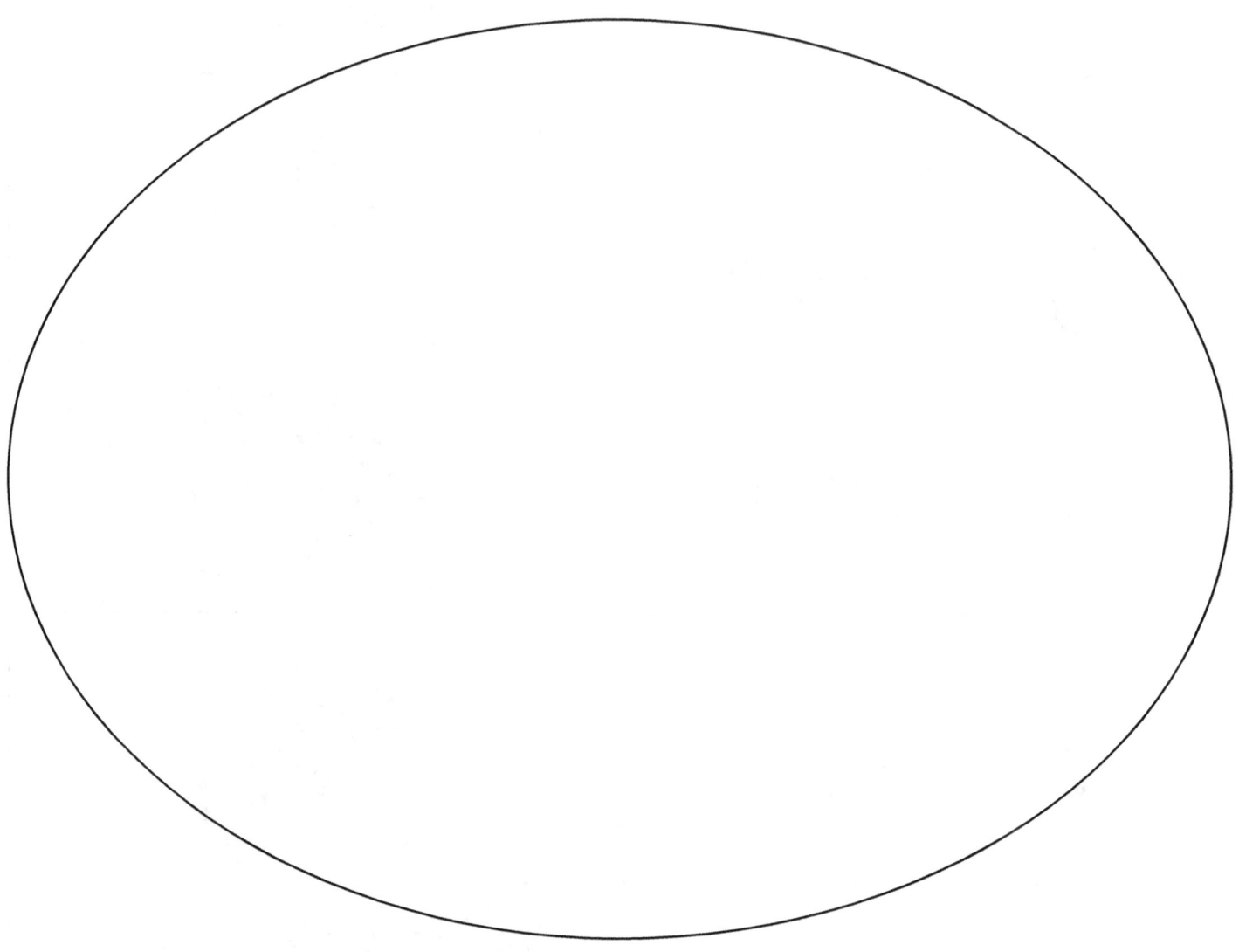

un oeuf	an egg	**le lait**	milk
la farine	flour	**le beurre**	butter
du sel	salt		

Extra!

How many pancake toppings can you name, in French?

Mardi gras

Puzzle page

Cherche les mots dans la grille.
Search for the words in the grid.

Mardi gras
crêpe
oeuf
lait
farine
beurre
sel
poêle
fête
masque
défilé
char

```
x  m  a  s  q  u  e  c  r  e
o  m  a  r  d  i  g  r  a  s
c  h  a  r  k  m  o  ê  n  o
l  o  p  i  b  l  o  p  l  e
f  a  r  i  n  e  g  e  m  u
l  o  i  p  p  l  u  n  g  f
o  k  j  t  o  m  b  r  i  g
k  l  i  f  ê  t  e  z  r  a
d  é  f  i  l  é  m  b  o  e
p  o  ê  l  e  v  s  e  l  d
```

Remets les lettres dans l'ordre.
Put the letters in order.

neu rêepc   *une crêpe*
el eburre   ....
ud les   ....
al friean   ....
nu fueo   ....
el tail   ....

Relie les mots et les images.
Match the words and pictures.

A   B   C

une crêpe   ....
un oeuf   ....
le lait   ....

Qu'est-ce que c'est?
What is it?

_ _ _ / _ _ ê _ _   *une crêpe*
_ _ e / _ _ ê _ _
_ _ / _ _ _ t
d _ / _ _ l
_ _ / o _ _ _

Mardi gras

Sentence building

Mime making a pancake using the recipe below.

Mettez le tamis au dessus du saladier.	Put the sieve on top of the bowl.
Mettez la farine dans le tamis et dans le saladier.	Put the flour in the sieve and into the bowl.
Ajoutez une pincée de sel.	Add a little salt.
Mettez deux oeufs dans un autre saladier.	Put two eggs in another bowl.
Mettez du lait dans ce saladier.	Put the milk in this bowl.
Mettez les oeufs et le lait dans le saladier avec la farine.	Put the eggs and the milk in the bowl with the flour.
Mélangez.	Mix together.

Make a shopping list for pancakes.

Il y a un oeuf, du lait, du sel ...   There is an egg, milk, salt ...

Make a recipe card for pancakes.

ajoutez	add
mélangez	mix
cuisinez	cook

Joyeuses Pâques

Key vocabulary

Joyeuses Pâques	Happy Easter
le lapin de Pâques	the Easter Bunny
un oeuf de Pâques	an Easter Egg
du chocolat	chocolate
un panier	a basket
une jonquille	a daffodil
un agneau	a lamb
un poussin	a chick
une cloche	a bell
une église	a church
la chasse aux oeufs	an Easter Egg hunt
le printemps	spring

Joyeuses Pâques ✂ Matching cards

Joyeuses Pâques	**Happy Easter**
un lapin	a rabbit
du chocolat	chocolate
un oeuf	an egg
un panier	a basket
une jonquille	a daffodil

Joyeuses Pâques Matching cards

un agneau	a lamb
un poussin	a chick
une cloche	a bell
une église	a church
la chasse aux oeufs	an Easter Egg hunt
le printemps	spring

Joyeuses Pâques — Picture cards

Joyeuses Pâques	
un lapin	
du chocolat	
un oeuf	
un panier	
une jonquille	

Joyeuses Pâques — ✂ Picture cards

un agneau	
un poussin	
une cloche	
une église	
la chasse aux oeufs	
le printemps	

Joyeuses Pâques   Activity sheet

Nom: ....   Date: ....

I know some Easter words in French.

Draw the Easter objects described below. Take care to colour them the right colour!

un lapin bleu	*une cloche verte*	*une jonquille jaune*
un agneau blanc	*un poussin jaune*	*un panier rouge*
le chocolat marron	*une église noire*	*une cloche d'or*

Extra!

Design **un bonnet de Pâques** (an Easter bonnet) on the back of this sheet.

Joyeuses Pâques

Puzzle page

Cherche les mots dans la grille.
Search for the words in the grid.

lapin
oeuf de Pâques
chocolat
panier
jonquille
agneau
poussin
cloche
église
printemps

```
e  a  s  f  p  a  n  i  e  r  j  p
c  l  o  g  é  g  l  i  s  e  m  o
l  o  k  l  e  n  g  o  n  g  u
o  e  u  f  d  e  p  â  q  u  e  s
c  g  c  f  c  a  h  u  c  e  g  s
h  k  l  o  c  u  m  e  a  s  g  i
e  j  o  n  q  u  i  l  l  e  n  n
m  o  l  a  p  i  n  p  l  i  b  g
c  h  o  c  o  l  a  t  q  u  i  f
s  t  o  p  r  i  n  t  e  m  p  s
```

Remets les lettres dans l'ordre.
Put the letters in order.

nu ilpan	*un lapin*
ud otlccaho	....
nu irpnae	....
nu sspiuon	....
nu eanuga	....
el mnepstirp	....

Devine qui?
Guess who?

A yellow flower.	*une jonquille*
I hop.	....
I'm yellow and fluffy.	....
I ring.	....
I'm delicious.	....

Joyeuses Pâques — Sentence building

Describe Easter using 'il y a …'
Il y a le lapin de Pâques, des œufs de Pâques …
There is the Easter Bunny, Easter eggs …

Make an Easter card.

Joyeuses Pâques!	Happy Easter
Chère Maman	Dear Mum
Cher Papa	Dear Dad
Bisous	Love from

JOYEUSES PÂQUES

Halloween

Key vocabulary

un fantôme	a ghost
un crâne	a skull
un déguisement	a costume
un vampire	a vampire
un chat noir	a black cat
un squelette	a skeleton
une maison hantée	a haunted house
une sorcière	a witch
une araignée	a spider
des bonbons	sweets
une citrouille	a pumpkin
une chauve-souris	a bat

Halloween — Matching cards

un fantôme	a ghost
un crâne	a skull
un déguisement	a costume
un vampire	a vampire
une maison hantée	a haunted house
une sorcière	a witch

Halloween ✂ Matching cards

un chat noir	a black cat
un squelette	a skeleton
des bonbons	sweets
une araignée	a spider
une citrouille	a pumpkin
une chauve-souris	a bat

Halloween ✂ Picture cards

un fantôme	
un crâne	
un déguisement	
un vampire	
une maison hantée	
une sorcière	

Halloween

✂ Picture cards

un chat noir	
un squelette	
des bonbons	
une araignée	
une citrouille	
une chauve-souris	

145

Halloween — Activity sheet

Nom: .... Date: ....

I know some Halloween words in French.

Draw the outline of a large haunted house below. Then draw and label some spooky Halloween objects inside it. Use the vocabulary box to help you.

un fantôme	a ghost	**un crâne**	a skull
un déguisement	a costume	**un vampire**	a vampire
un chat noir	a black cat	**un squelette**	a skeleton
une chauve-souris	a bat	**une sorcière**	a witch
une citrouille	a pumpkin	**une araignée**	a spider
des bonbons	sweets	**une maison hantée**	a haunted house

Halloween — Puzzle page

Cherche les mots dans la grille.
Search for the words in the grid.

fantôme
crâne
déguisement
vampire
chat noir
squelette
maison hantée
sorcière
araignée
bonbons
citrouille

```
m a i s o n h a n t é e
c l o b o n b o n s t s
h o o h a r b l i n g q
a c r â n e c l o d s u
t c i t r o u i l l e e
n i n b l o p r è r e l
o m k i v a m p i r e e
i n a r a i g n é e e t
r d é g u i s e m e n t
z f a n t ô m e p l u e
```

Remets les lettres dans l'ordre.
Put the letters in order.

eun lclioutrie — une citrouille
nu tsteteluqe — ....
sde bsobnon — ....
nu htca irno — ....
nu ipvmear — ....
eun èicreros — ....

Qu'est-ce que c'est?
What is it?

_ _ / f _ _ _ ô _ _   un fantôme
_ _ e / _ _ _ c _ _ _ e
_ _ / _ _ _ t / _ o _ _
u _ / a _ _ _ g _ _ _
_ n / c _ _ _ _

Relie les mots et les images.
Match the words and pictures.

A   B   C

un fantôme — ....
une sorcière — ....
une citrouille — ....

Devine qui?
Guess who?

I ride on my broomstick. — une sorcière
I am a black animal. — ....
I am orange. — ....
I have some big teeth. — ....
I live in a web. — ....

© Nicolette Hannam, Michelle Williams and Brilliant Publications. Bonne Idée.

Halloween — Sentence building

Describe the haunted house you have drawn on the activity sheet
Dans ma maison hantée, il y a …   In my haunted house there is …

Charades
Children could pull a Halloween word out of a hat and mime the word. Children are to guess it using French:

C'est un vampire?   Is it a vampire?

Oui/Non.   Yes/No

Write a song
Children could write a spooky song listing Halloween words, to the tune of 'Head, shoulders, knees and toes'. They could add their own actions and perform it to the class.

Ages: 5–11yrs

Loto Français

A Fun Way to Reinforce French Vocabulary

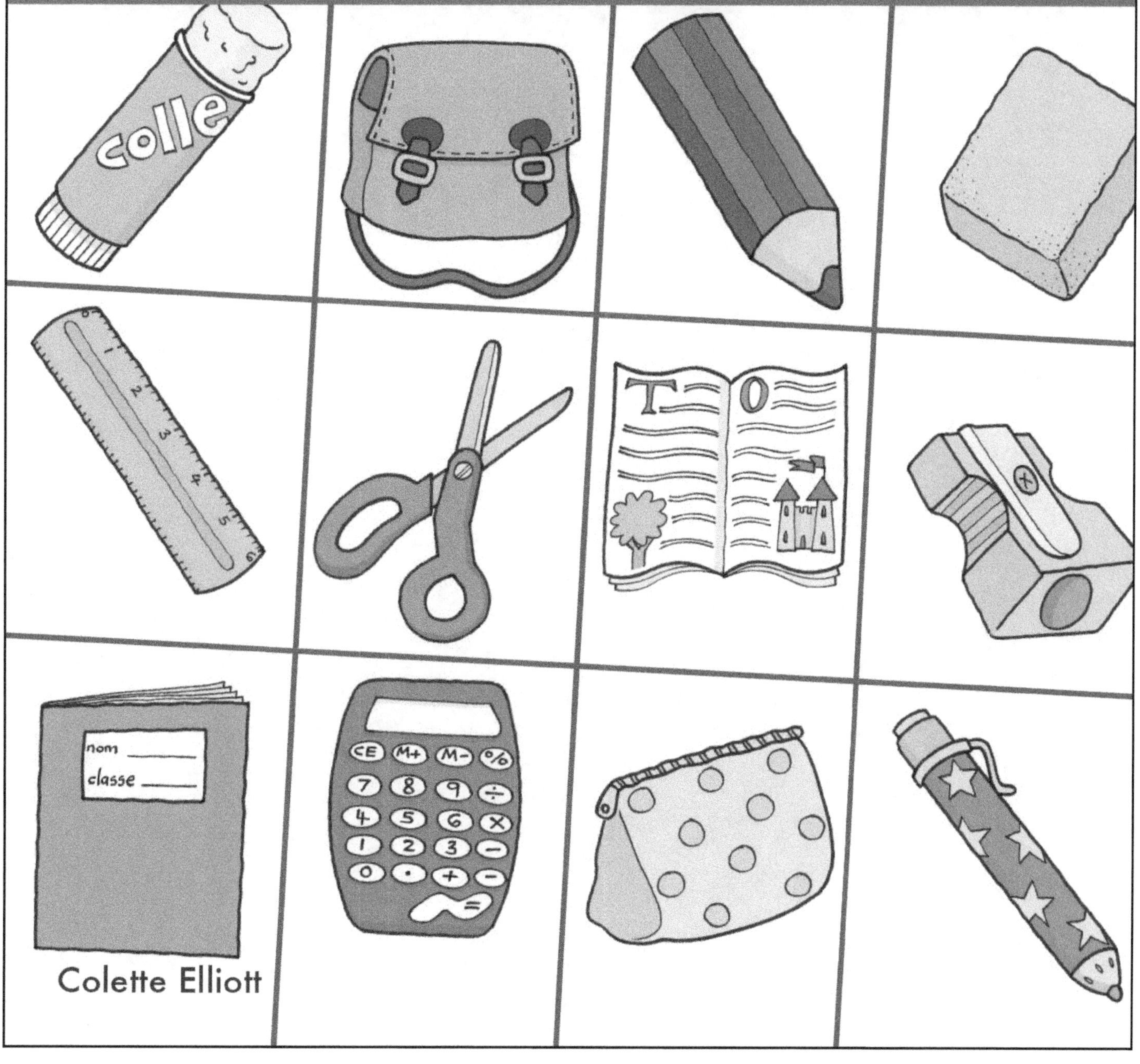

Colette Elliott

Loto Français

A Fun Way to Reinforce French Vocabulary

Colette Elliott

We hope you and your pupils enjoy playing the lotto games in this book. Brilliant Publications publishes many other books for teaching modern foreign languages. To find out more details on any of the titles listed below, please log onto our website: www.brilliantpublications.co.uk.

100+ Fun Ideas for Practising Modern Foreign Languages in the Primary Classroom	978-1-903853-98-6
More Fun Ideas for Advancing Modern Foreign Languages in the Primary Classroom	978-1-905780-72-3
Chantez Plus Fort!	978-1-903853-37-5
Hexagonie 1	978-1-905780-59-4
Hexagonie 2	978-1-905780-18-1
Jouons Tous Ensemble	978-1-903853-81-8
C'est Français!	978-1-903853-02-3
J'aime Chanter!	978-1-905780-11-2
J'aime Parler!	978-1-905780-12-9
French Pen Pals Made Easy	978-1-905780-10-5
French Festivals and Traditions	978-1-905780-44-0
Bonne Idée	978-1-905780-62-4
Unforgettable French	978-1-78317-093-7
¡Es Español!	978-1-903853-64-1
Juguemos Todos Juntos	978-1-903853-95-5
¡Vamos a Cantar!	978-1-905780-13-6
Spanish Pen Pals Made Easy	978-1-905780-42-3
Lotto en Español	978-1-905780-47-1
Spanish Festivals and Traditions	978-1-905780-53-2
Buena Idea	978-1-905780-63-1
Das ist Deutsch	978-1-905780-15-0
Wir Spielen Zusammen	978-1-903853-97-9
German Pen Pals Made Easy	978-1-905780-43-3
Deutsch-Lotto	978-1-905780-46-4
German Festivals and Traditions	978-1-905780-52-5
Gute Idee	978-1-905780-65-5
Giochiamo Tutti Insieme	978-1-903853-96-2
Lotto in Italiano	978-1-905780-48-8
Buon'Idea	978-1-905780-64-8

Published by Brilliant Publications
Unit 10
Sparrow Hall Farm
Edlesborough
Dunstable
Bedfordshire
LU6 2ES, UK

General information enquiries:
Tel: 01525 222292

The name Brilliant Publications and the logo are registered trademarks.

Written by Colette Elliott
Illustrated by Gaynor Berry
Front cover designed by Brilliant Publications

© Text Colette Elliott 2009
© Design Brilliant Publications 2009

Printed ISBN: 978-1-905780-45-7
e-pdf ISBN: 978-1-905780-98-3

First printed and published in the UK in 2009

The right of Colette Elliott to be identified as the author of this work has been asserted by herself in accordance with the Copyright, Designs and Patents Act 1988.

Pages 7–57 may be photocopied by individual teachers acting on behalf of the purchasing institution for classroom use only, without permission from the publisher and without declaration to the Copyright Licensing Agency or Publishers' Licensing Services. The materials may not be reproduced in any other form or for any other purpose without the prior permission of the publisher.

Contents

Introduction 4
How to play 5
Different ways of playing/ideas 6

Les nombres 1 à 12 (Numbers 1–12)
Call sheet 8
Picture only boards 9–10
Pictures and words boards 11–12
Words only boards 13–14

Les nombres 1 à 60 (Numbers 1–60)
Call sheet 15
Picture only boards 16–17
Pictures and words boards 18–19
Words only boards 20–21

Les animaux (Animals)
Call sheet 22
Picture only boards 23–24
Pictures and words boards 25–26
Words only boards 27–28

Bon appétit! (Food)
Call sheet 29
Picture only boards 30–31
Pictures and words boards 32–33
Words only boards 34–35

En classe (Classroom objects)
Call sheet 36
Picture only boards 37–38
Pictures and words boards 39–40
Words only boards 41–42

Les vêtements (Clothes)
Call sheet 43
Picture only boards 44–45
Pictures and words boards 46–47
Words only boards 48–49

Noël (Christmas)
Call sheet 50
Picture only boards 51–52
Pictures and words boards 53–54
Words only boards 55–56

Blank template boards 57
List of vocabulary used in games 58

Introduction

The perennially popular game of lotto (or 'loto' as it is called in French) is an enjoyable and effective way to teach and/or reinforce vocabulary and language structures. It can be used as a teaching tool or as a fun follow-up activity after a lesson. It provides a stimulating and meaningful way to develop reading, listening and speaking skills.

The games in *Loto Français* can be played in a variety of ways (see pages 5–7) and with very little preparation from you. There is no need to give the children counters or individual cards. Simply photocopy the boards, hand them out to your pupils together with some colouring pencils and, bingo, you can start playing!

Our unique call sheets provide the 'order of call' and enable you to follow the game closely and to select which team you want to win.

Lotto can be played in small groups, or with an entire class. There is no limit to the number of players and the games are suitable for ages four upwards.

There are seven topics in *Loto Français*:
- Les nombres 1–12   Numbers 1–12
- Les nombres 1–60   Numbers 1–60
- Les animaux   Animals
- Bon appétit!   Food
- En classe   Classroom objects
- Les vêtements   Clothes
- Noël   Christmas

For each topic there are three versions of the boards, allowing maximum flexibility, particularly in mixed ability classes.

pictures only

words and pictures

words only

The ideas in this book are by no means exhaustive and, should you decide to cut the boards to make flashcards or playing cards, then the number of games is unlimited!

Have fun playing!

How to play

Getting started
For each topic, in each format, there are four different numbered boards, so you can play with four teams. Just photocopy the sheets, cut them in half, and hand out the boards to the children. For a class of 28 pupils, you only need to copy two pages seven times each.

It is a good idea to go through the vocabulary with the children before playing. The best way to do this is either to scan and place the four boards on the whiteboard, or enlarge the 12 pictures on the photocopier and use them as flashcards.

Make sure that the boards are evenly distributed throughout the class. After giving the boards out and before you start playing, ask for a show of hands to see how the teams are spread out in the classroom. The children like to see who is in their team and this increases the element of competition!

How to play
Each topic contains a call sheet, with the words numbered 1 to 12. The caller can start calling from any number. The white area in the table indicates who the winning board will be.

The children can play on their own or in pairs for moral support.

The winner is the first child to shout 'loto' (hopefully the rest of that team will also shout 'loto', but the real winner is the child who shouts out first). Get the winner to say all the words in French whilst you check on the list. This is a good reading/speaking exercise.

Once the first team has won, you can stop the game or carry on until everyone has shouted 'loto' (you will know from the call sheet who the next winner will be).

You can play several games with the same boards by marking the boards in different ways:
◆ Colour the box outline (or only one side of the box if you want to make it last!)
◆ Colour the picture
◆ Colour the background
◆ Tick or cross the box, etc.

It is best to tell the children to shout 'loto' as soon as the caller says the word, rather than wait until the colouring is done, to avoid any arguments.

Variations
Instead of evenly distributing the boards, you could make it a competition within the class: divide the class into four groups, give the same boards to each group, and see which group says 'loto' first.

Children could play in groups of five. One child is the caller (give him/her a photocopy of the call list) and the others use four different boards. Only one winner this time!

The order of call is the same for all the topics, so you can play 'mix and match' games with different topics. If you decide to do so, make sure that the four different teams are evenly spread.

Different ways of playing/ideas

- Call the words from the call sheet in French. Start anywhere, but make a note of where you started either on a photocopy of the call sheet or on a separate sheet of paper. Alternatively, get a child to do the calling. Assist him/her with the more difficult words.

- The children take it in turns to call out an item from their own board in French. When they call a word, they colour their own picture and everybody who has that picture says 'merci' and colours their picture. Then the child sitting next to the caller says the next word, etc. This is a very good reading exercise if the 'words only' boards are used. The teacher should make a note of which items have been called on the call sheet.

- Call the words in English, and the children have to find the French translation (this can only be played using the 'words only' boards).

- Show a picture without saying anything (using the 'words only' boards).

- Write a word on the board without saying anything (for 'pictures only' boards).

- Instead of using the call sheets, photocopy the boards and cut them up into cards, then pick the cards out of a hat. The pupils could take turns to pick a card and call out the word.

- Ask the children to colour the pictures before playing and then call the words with a colour, eg "un chat rouge". To keep the game from lasting too long, limit the children to the same two colours. (You can use the two columns on the call sheets to indicate the colour. For example, write B for "bleu" at the top of the list of French words and R for "rouge" at the top of the English word list.)

- Give a description of the word in French.

- For the number "loto" boards, give sums for the children to work out.

- Spell the words.

- Give a rhyming word.

- Include the word in a sentence eg un bonbon; un bonbon s'il vous plaît; je voudrais un bonbon s'il vous plaît; bonjour madame, je voudrais un bonbon s'il vous plaît.

- . Make the game last the whole lesson. Give the boards at the beginning and call the words at intervals during the lesson, either on their own or in a sentence.

- Give everybody the same board. Each child has to preselect four items by circling or colouring them.

- Give the children the blank template board (pages 57) and get them to write/draw their own items/numbers from a list you have given on the board. This can be played with any topic/structures/verbs/grammar.

- Make the children repeat the word several times whilst they are colouring.

- The children ask a question each time, eg:

  * Qu'est-ce que vous avez? — What do you have?

  * Combien? Quel numéro? — How many? What number?
    Vous avez quel numéro? — What number do you have?

  * Qu'est-ce que c'est? — What is this?

  * Qu'est-ce que vous mangez? — What are you eating?

  * Vous avez un animal? — Do you have an animal?

  * Qu'est-ce que vous portez? — What are you wearing?

- If you photocopy the boards double-sided, they will last even longer.

Les nombres de 1 à 12

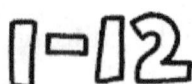

Team 1 to win	Start on 2 or 7
Team 2 to win	Start on 1, 3, 4 or 12
Team 3 to win	Start on 3, 5, 7, 10 or 11
Team 4 to win	Start on 5, 7, 8 or 9
All teams to win	Start on 6

These numbers refer to the numbers on the left and right of the grid below.

Tick the white boxes in the grid as you call out the words.

				Winning team									
				2	1	2&3	2	3&4	All	1,3,4	4	4	3	3	2	
Order of call	1	cinq	five													1
	2	neuf	nine													2
	3	onze	eleven													3
	4	deux	two													4
	5	quatre	four													5
	6	douze	twelve													6
	7	trois	three													7
	8	un	one													8
	9	six	six													9
	10	huit	eight													10
	11	dix	ten													11
	12	sept	seven													12
	1	cinq	five													1
	2	neuf	nine													2
	3	onze	eleven													3
	4	deux	two													4
	5	quatre	four													5
	6	douze	twelve													6
	7	trois	three													7
	8	un	one													8
	9	six	six													9

Loto! (Équipe 1) Nom: _____ 1-12

2	8	9
3	1	4

Loto Français – Les nombres de 1 à 12

Loto! (Équipe 2) Nom: _____ 1-12

1	5	6
4	12	2

Loto Français – Les nombres de 1 à 12

Loto! (Équipe 3) Nom: _____ 1-12

7	5	10
11	3	4

Loto Français – Les nombres de 1 à 12

Loto! (Équipe 4) Nom: _____ 1-12

11	4	6
7	8	9

Loto! (Équipe 1) Nom: _____   1-12

2 deux	8 huit	9 neuf
3 trois	1 un	4 quatre

Loto Français – Les nombres de 1 à 12   © Colette Elliott and Brilliant Publications. This board may be photocopied for use by the purchaser.

Loto! (Équipe 2) Nom: _____   1-12

1 un	5 cinq	6 six
4 quatre	12 douze	2 deux

Loto Français – Les nombres de 1 à 12   © Colette Elliott and Brilliant Publications. This board may be photocopied for use by the purchaser.

Loto! (Équipe 3)   Nom: _____   1-12

7 sept	**5** cinq	**10** dix
11 onze	**3** trois	**4** quatre

Loto Français – Les nombres de 1 à 12

Loto! (Équipe 4)   Nom: _____   1-12

11 onze	**4** quatre	**6** six
7 sept	**8** huit	**9** neuf

Loto! (Équipe 1)   Nom: _____   1-12

deux	huit	neuf
trois	un	quatre

Loto Français – Les nombres de 1 à 12

Loto! (Équipe 2)   Nom: _____   1-12

un	cinq	six
quatre	douze	deux

Loto Français – Les nombres de 1 à 12

Loto! (Équipe 3)   Nom: _____   1-12

sept	cinq	dix
onze	trois	quatre

Loto Français – Les nombres de 1 à 12

Loto! (Équipe 4)   Nom: _____   1-12

onze	quatre	six
sept	huit	neuf

Les nombres de 1 à 60

Team 1 to win	Start on 2 or 7
Team 2 to win	Start on 1, 3, 4 or 12
Team 3 to win	Start on 3, 5, 7, 10 or 11
Team 4 to win	Start on 5, 7, 8 or 9
All teams to win	Start on 6

These numbers refer to the numbers on the left and right of the grid below.

Tick the white boxes in the grid as you call out the words.

				Winning team										
				2	1	2&3	2	3&4	All	1,3,4	4	4	3	3	2	
Order of call	1	vingt-six	twenty-six													1
	2	sept	seven													2
	3	soixante	sixty													3
	4	trente-cinq	thirty-five													4
	5	cinquante-huit	fifty-eight													5
	6	quarante et un	forty-one													6
	7	quinze	fifteen													7
	8	cinquante	fifty													8
	9	douze	twelve													9
	10	quarante-deux	forty-two													10
	11	trente-quatre	thirty-four													11
	12	dix-neuf	nineteen													12
	1	vingt-six	twenty-six													1
	2	sept	seven													2
	3	soixante	sixty													3
	4	trente-cinq	thirty-five													4
	5	cinquante-huit	fifty-eight													5
	6	quarante et un	forty-one													6
	7	quinze	fifteen													7
	8	cinquante	fifty													8
	9	douze	twelve													9

Loto Français

Loto! (Équipe 1) Nom: _____ 1-60

35	42	7
15	50	58

Loto Français – Les nombres de 1 à 60   © Colette Elliott and Brilliant Publications. This board may be photocopied for use by the purchaser.

Loto! (Équipe 2) Nom: _____ 1-60

50	26	12
58	41	35

Loto Français – Les nombres de 1 à 60   © Colette Elliott and Brilliant Publications. This board may be photocopied for use by the purchaser.

Loto! (Équipe 3)   Nom: _____   1-60

19	26	34
60	15	58

Loto Français – Les nombres de 1 à 60

Loto! (Équipe 4)   Nom: _____   1-60

60	58	12
19	42	7

Loto Français – Les nombres de 1 à 60

Loto! (Équipe 1) Nom: _____   1-60

35 trente-cinq	**42** quarante-deux	**7** sept
15 quinze	**50** cinquante	**58** cinquante-huit

Loto Français – Les nombres de 1 à 60   © Colette Elliott and Brilliant Publications. This board may be photocopied for use by the purchaser.

Loto! (Équipe 2) Nom: _____   1-60

50 cinquante	**26** vingt-six	**12** douze
58 cinquante-huit	**41** quarante et un	**35** trente-cinq

Loto Français – Les nombres de 1 à 60   © Colette Elliott and Brilliant Publications. This board may be photocopied for use by the purchaser.

Loto! (Équipe 3) Nom: _____   1-60

19 dix-neuf	**26** vingt-six	**34** trente-quatre
60 soixante	**15** quinze	**58** cinquante-huit

Loto Français – Les nombres de 1 à 60

Loto! (Équipe 4) Nom: _____   1-60

60 soixante	**58** cinquante-huit	**12** douze
19 dix-neuf	**42** quarante-deux	**7** sept

Loto Français – Les nombres de 1 à 60

Loto! (Équipe 1)　Nom: _____　1-60

trente-cinq	quarante-deux	sept
quinze	cinquante	cinquante-huit

Loto Français – Les nombres de 1 à 60　© Colette Elliott and Brilliant Publications. This board may be photocopied for use by the purchaser.

Loto! (Équipe 2)　Nom: _____　1-60

cinquante	vingt-six	douze
cinquante-huit	quarante et un	trente-cinq

Loto Français – Les nombres de 1 à 60　© Colette Elliott and Brilliant Publications. This board may be photocopied for use by the purchaser.

Loto! (Équipe 3)   Nom: _____   1-60

dix-neuf	vingt-six	trente-quatre
soixante	quinze	cinquante-huit

Loto Français – Les nombres de 1 à 60

Loto! (Équipe 4)   Nom: _____   1-60

soixante	cinquante-huit	douze
dix-neuf	quarante-deux	sept

Les animaux

Team 1 to win	Start on 2 or 7
Team 2 to win	Start on 1, 3, 4 or 12
Team 3 to win	Start on 3, 5, 7, 10 or 11
Team 4 to win	Start on 5, 7, 8 or 9
All teams to win	Start on 6

These numbers refer to the numbers on the left and right of the grid below.

Tick the white boxes in the grid as you call out the words.

				Winning team										
				2	1	2&3	2	3&4	All	1,3,4	4	4	3	3	2	
Order of call	1	un cochon	a pig													1
	2	une souris	a mouse													2
	3	un cochon d'Inde	a guinea pig													3
	4	une vache	a cow													4
	5	un hamster	a hamster													5
	6	un cheval	a horse													6
	7	un lapin	a rabbit													7
	8	un chat	a cat													8
	9	un chien	a dog													9
	10	un poisson rouge	a goldfish													10
	11	un canard	a duck													11
	12	une poule	a hen													12
	1	un cochon	a pig													1
	2	une souris	a mouse													2
	3	un cochon d'Inde	a guinea pig													3
	4	une vache	a cow													4
	5	un hamster	a hamster													5
	6	un cheval	a horse													6
	7	un lapin	a rabbit													7
	8	un chat	a cat													8
	9	un chien	a dog													9

Loto Français

Loto! (Équipe 1)   Nom: _____

Loto Français – Les animaux   © Colette Elliott and Brilliant Publications. This board may be photocopied for use by the purchaser.

Loto! (Équipe 2)   Nom: _____

Loto Français – Les animaux   © Colette Elliott and Brilliant Publications. This board may be photocopied for use by the purchaser.   23

Loto! (Équipe 3)   Nom: _____

Loto Français – Les animaux   © Colette Elliott and Brilliant Publications. This board may be photocopied for use by the purchaser.

Loto! (Équipe 4)   Nom: _____

24   Loto Français – Les animaux   © Colette Elliott and Brilliant Publications. This board may be photocopied for use by the purchaser.

Loto! (Équipe 1) Nom: _____

 une vache	 un poisson rouge	 une souris
 un lapin	 un chat	 un hamster

Loto Français – Les animaux   © Colette Elliott and Brilliant Publications. This board may be photocopied for use by the purchaser.

Loto! (Équipe 2) Nom: _____

 un chat	 un cochon	 un chien
 un hamster	 un cheval	 une vache

Loto Français – Les animaux   © Colette Elliott and Brilliant Publications. This board may be photocopied for use by the purchaser.

Loto! (Équipe 3)   Nom: _____

 une poule	 un cochon	 un canard
 un cochon d'Inde	 un lapin	 un hamster

Loto Français – Les animaux

Loto! (Équipe 4)   Nom: _____

 un cochon d'Inde	 un hamster	 un chien
 une poule	 un poisson rouge	 une souris

Loto! (Équipe 1) Nom: _____

une vache	un poisson rouge	une souris
un lapin	un chat	un hamster

Loto Français – Les animaux

Loto! (Équipe 2) Nom: _____

un chat	un cochon	un chien
un hamster	un cheval	une vache

Loto Français – Les animaux

Loto! (Équipe 3) Nom: _____

une poule	un cochon	un canard
un cochon d'Inde	un lapin	un hamster

Loto Français – Les animaux

© Colette Elliott and Brilliant Publications. This board may be photocopied for use by the purchaser.

Loto! (Équipe 4) Nom: _____

un cochon d'Inde	un hamster	un chien
une poule	un poisson rouge	une souris

Bon appétit!

Team 1 to win	Start on 2 or 7
Team 2 to win	Start on 1, 3, 4 or 12
Team 3 to win	Start on 3, 5, 7, 10 or 11
Team 4 to win	Start on 5, 7, 8 or 9
All teams to win	Start on 6

These numbers refer to the numbers on the left and right of the grid below.

Tick the white boxes in the grid as you call out the words.

				Winning team										
				2	1	2&3	2	3&4	All	1,3,4	4	4	3	3	2	
Order of call	1	un gâteau	a cake													1
	2	une pomme	an apple													2
	3	une glace	an ice-cream													3
	4	du fromage	(some) cheese													4
	5	un poulet	a chicken													5
	6	une pomme de terre	a potato													6
	7	du lait	(some) milk													7
	8	du jambon	(some) ham													8
	9	un œuf	an egg													9
	10	des frites	(some) chips													10
	11	du pain	(some) bread													11
	12	des bonbons	(some) sweets													12
	1	un gâteau	a cake													1
	2	une pomme	an apple													2
	3	une glace	an ice-cream													3
	4	du fromage	(some) cheese													4
	5	un poulet	a chicken													5
	6	une pomme de terre	a potato													6
	7	du lait	(some) milk													7
	8	du jambon	(some) ham													8
	9	un œuf	an egg													9

Loto! (Équipe 1)   Nom: _____

	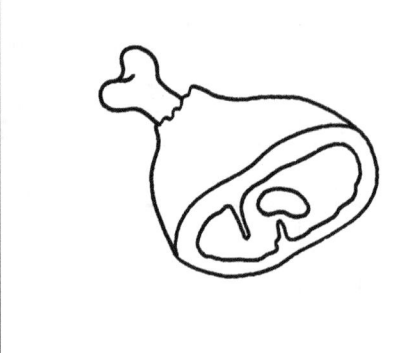	

Loto Français – Bon appétit!   © Colette Elliott and Brilliant Publications. This board may be photocopied for use by the purchaser.

Loto! (Équipe 2)   Nom: _____

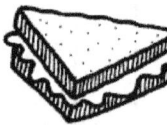

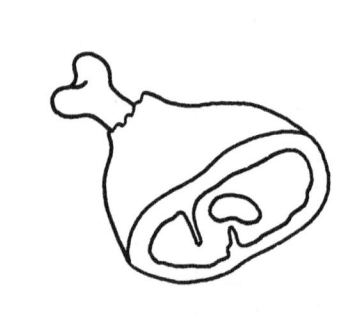		
	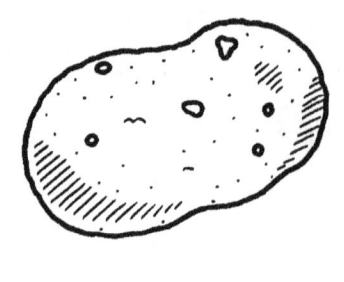	

Loto Français – Bon appétit!   © Colette Elliott and Brilliant Publications. This board may be photocopied for use by the purchaser.

Loto! (Équipe 3)   Nom: _____

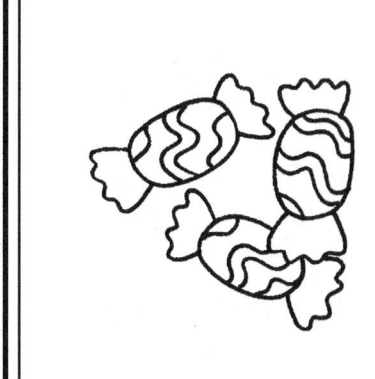  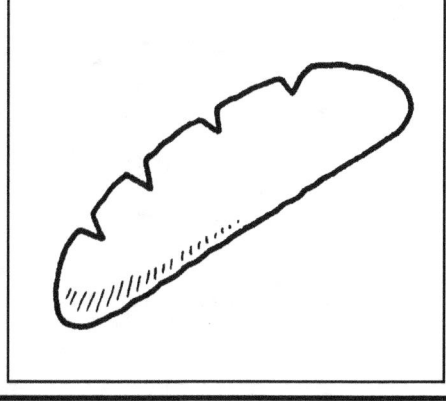

Loto Français – Bon appétit! © Colette Elliott and Brilliant Publications. This board may be photocopied for use by the purchaser.

Loto! (Équipe 4)   Nom: _____

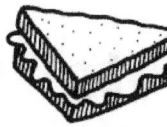

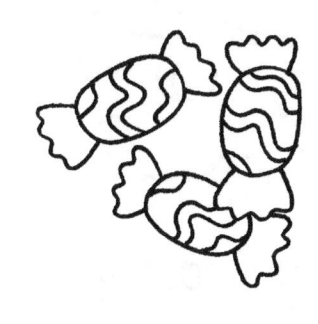  

Loto Français – Bon appétit! © Colette Elliott and Brilliant Publications. This board may be photocopied for use by the purchaser.

Loto! (Équipe 1)   Nom: _____

du fromage	des frites	une pomme
	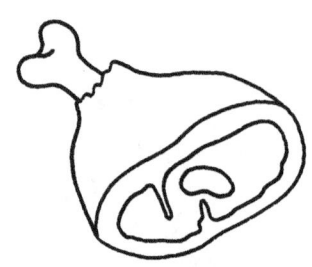	
du lait	du jambon	un poulet

Loto Français – Bon appétit!   © Colette Elliott and Brilliant Publications. This board may be photocopied for use by the purchaser.

Loto! (Équipe 2)   Nom: _____

du jambon	un gâteau	un œuf
	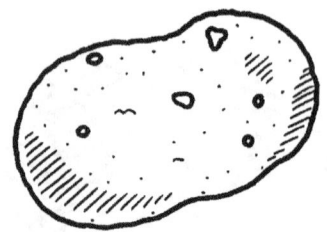	
un poulet	une pomme de terre	du fromage

Loto! (Équipe 3) Nom: _____

 des bonbons	 un gâteau	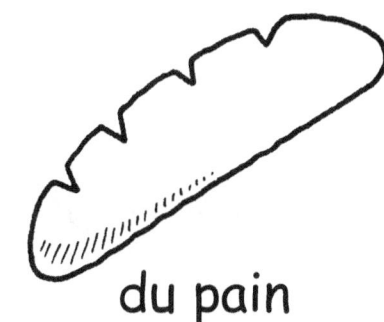 du pain
 une glace	 du lait	 un poulet

Loto Français – Bon appétit!   © Colette Elliott and Brilliant Publications. This board may be photocopied for use by the purchaser.

Loto! (Équipe 4) Nom: _____

 une glace	 un poulet	 un œuf
 des bonbons	 des frites	 une pomme

Loto Français – Bon appétit!   © Colette Elliott and Brilliant Publications. This board may be photocopied for use by the purchaser.

Loto! (Équipe 1) Nom: _____

du fromage	des frites	une pomme
du lait	du jambon	un poulet

Loto Français – Bon appétit!

Loto! (Équipe 2) Nom: _____

du jambon	un gâteau	un œuf
un poulet	une pomme de terre	du fromage

Loto Français – Bon appétit!

Loto! (Équipe 3)   Nom: _____

des bonbons	un gâteau	du pain
une glace	du lait	un poulet

Loto Français – Bon appétit!

Loto! (Équipe 4)   Nom: _____

une glace	un poulet	un œuf
des bonbons	des frites	une pomme

Loto Français – Bon appétit!

En classe

Team 1 to win	Start on 2 or 7
Team 2 to win	Start on 1, 3, 4 or 12
Team 3 to win	Start on 3, 5, 7, 10 or 11
Team 4 to win	Start on 5, 7, 8 or 9
All teams to win	Start on 6

These numbers refer to the numbers on the left and right of the grid below.

Tick the white boxes in the grid as you call out the words.

				Winning team										
				2	1	2&3	2	3&4	All	1,3,4	4	4	3	3	2	
Order of call	1	un livre	a book													1
	2	un taille-crayon	a pencil sharpener													2
	3	une règle	a ruler													3
	4	un cartable	a school bag													4
	5	des ciseaux	some scissors													5
	6	un crayon	a pencil													6
	7	une gomme	a rubber													7
	8	un cahier	an exercise book													8
	9	un stylo	a pen													9
	10	une trousse	a pencil case													10
	11	une calculatrice	a calculator													11
	12	un bâton de colle	a glue stick													12
	1	un livre	a book													1
	2	un taille-crayon	a pencil sharpener													2
	3	une règle	a ruler													3
	4	un cartable	a school bag													4
	5	des ciseaux	some scissors													5
	6	un crayon	a pencil													6
	7	une gomme	a rubber													7
	8	un cahier	an exercise book													8
	9	un stylo	a pen													9

Loto! (Équipe 1) Nom: _____

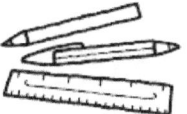

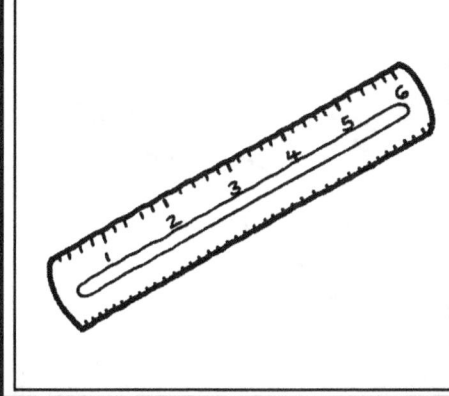		

Loto Français – En classe © Colette Elliott and Brilliant Publications. This board may be photocopied for use by the purchaser.

Loto! (Équipe 2) Nom: _____

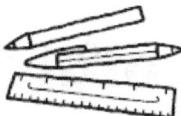

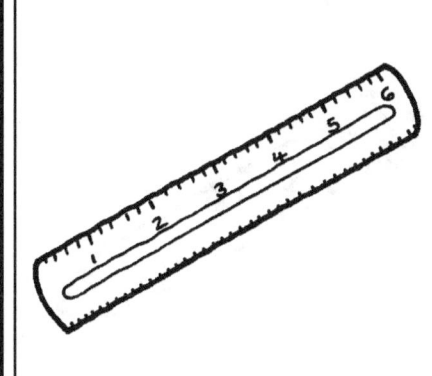		
		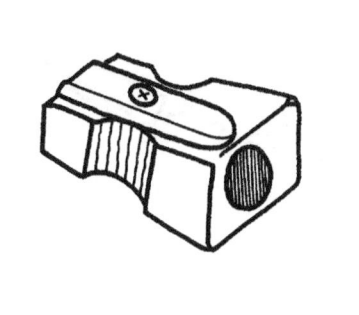

Loto Français – En classe © Colette Elliott and Brilliant Publications. This board may be photocopied for use by the purchaser.

Loto! (Équipe 3) Nom: _____

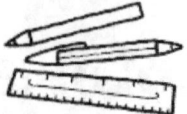

 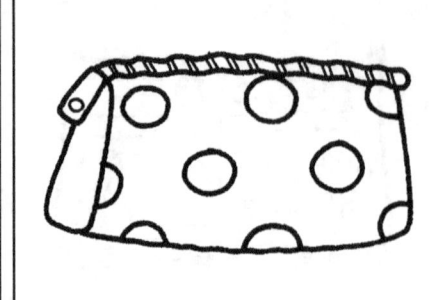 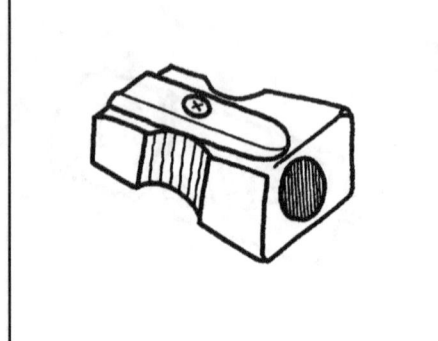

Loto Français – En classe   © Colette Elliott and Brilliant Publications. This board may be photocopied for use by the purchaser.

Loto! (Équipe 4) Nom: _____

Loto! (Équipe 1)   Nom: _____

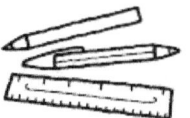

 un bâton de colle	 un livre	 une calculatrice
 une règle	 une gomme	 des ciseaux

Loto Français – En classe   © Colette Elliott and Brilliant Publications. This board may be photocopied for use by the purchaser.

Loto! (Équipe 2)   Nom: _____

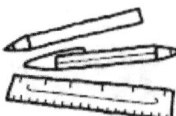

 une règle	 des ciseaux	 un stylo
 un bâton de colle	 une trousse	 un taille-crayon

Loto Français – En classe   © Colette Elliott and Brilliant Publications. This board may be photocopied for use by the purchaser.

Loto! (Équipe 3)   Nom: _____

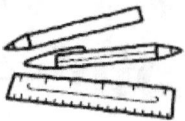

	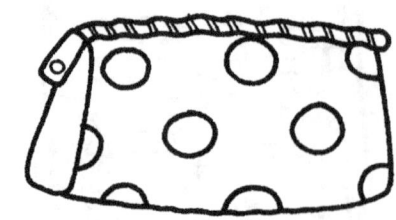	
un cartable	une trousse	un taille-crayon

une gomme	un cahier	des ciseaux

Loto Français – En classe © Colette Elliott and Brilliant Publications. This board may be photocopied for use by the purchaser.

Loto! (Équipe 4)   Nom: _____

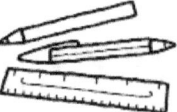

un cahier	un livre	un stylo
		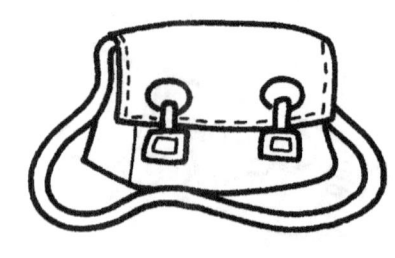
des ciseaux	un crayon	un cartable

Loto! (Équipe 1) Nom: _____

un bâton de colle	un livre	une calculatrice
une règle	une gomme	des ciseaux

Loto! (Équipe 2) Nom: _____

une règle	des ciseaux	un stylo
un bâton de colle	une trousse	un taille-crayon

Loto! (Équipe 3)   Nom: _____

un cartable	une trousse	un taille-crayon
une gomme	un cahier	des ciseaux

Loto! (Équipe 4)   Nom: _____

un cahier	un livre	un stylo
des ciseaux	un crayon	un cartable

Les vêtements

Team 1 to win	Start on 2 or 7
Team 2 to win	Start on 1, 3, 4 or 12
Team 3 to win	Start on 3, 5, 7, 10 or 11
Team 4 to win	Start on 5, 7, 8 or 9
All teams to win	Start on 6

These numbers refer to the numbers on the left and right of the grid below.

Tick the white boxes in the grid as you call out the words.

				Winning team											
				2	1	2&3	2	3&4	All	1,3,4	4	4	3	3	2	
Order of call	1	des chaussures	(some) shoes													1
	2	un pull	a jumper													2
	3	une robe	a dress													3
	4	un pantalon	trousers													4
	5	un jean	(a pair of) jeans													5
	6	un t-shirt	a T-shirt													6
	7	un chapeau	a hat													7
	8	une jupe	a skirt													8
	9	une chemise	a shirt													9
	10	une cravate	a tie													10
	11	des chaussettes	(some) socks													11
	12	un short	(a pair of) shorts													12
	1	des chaussures	(some) shoes													1
	2	un pull	a jumper													2
	3	une robe	a dress													3
	4	un pantalon	trousers													4
	5	un jean	(a pair of) jeans													5
	6	un t-shirt	a T-shirt													6
	7	un chapeau	a hat													7
	8	une jupe	a skirt													8
	9	une chemise	a shirt													9

Loto Français © Colette Elliott and Brilliant Publications. This board may be photocopied for use by the purchaser.

Loto! (Équipe 1)   Nom: _____

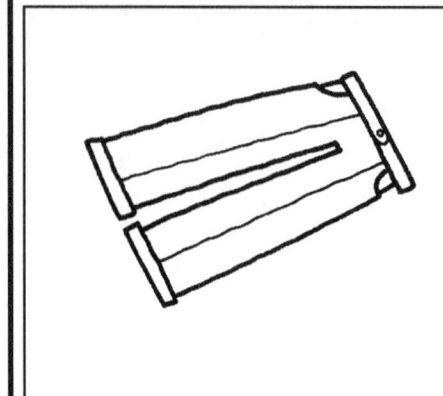 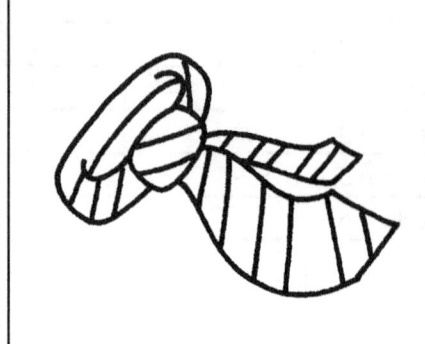 

 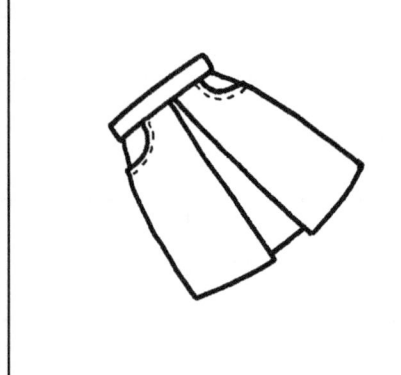 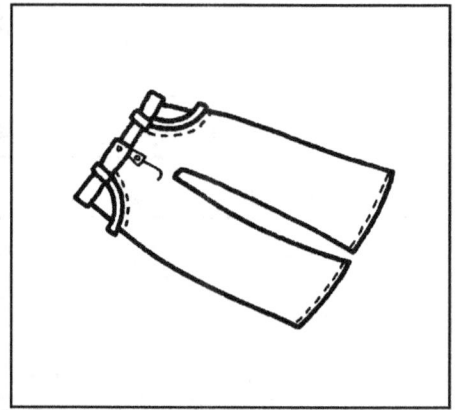

Loto Français – Les vêtements   © Colette Elliott and Brilliant Publications. This board may be photocopied for use by the purchaser.

Loto! (Équipe 2)   Nom: _____

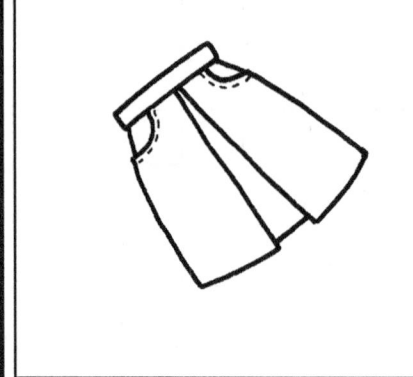  

Loto! (Équipe 3)   Nom: _____

  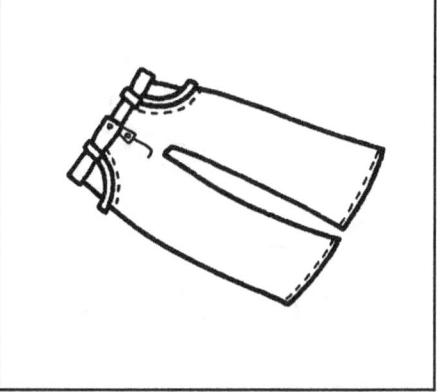

Loto Français – Les vêtements   © Colette Elliott and Brilliant Publications. This board may be photocopied for use by the purchaser.

Loto! (Équipe 4)   Nom: _____

 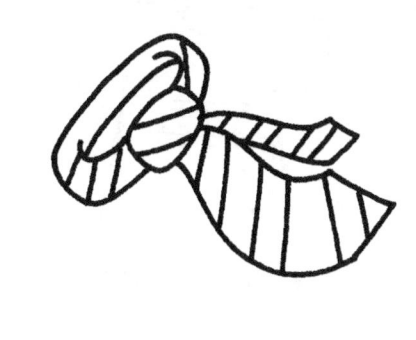 

Loto Français – Les vêtements   © Colette Elliott and Brilliant Publications. This board may be photocopied for use by the purchaser.

Loto! (Équipe 1) Nom: _____

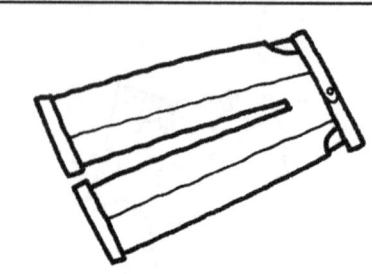		
un pantalon	une cravate	un pull

un chapeau	une jupe	un jean

Loto! (Équipe 2) Nom: _____

une jupe	des chaussures	une chemise

un jean	un t-shirt	un pantalon

Loto! (Équipe 3)   Nom: _____

 un short	 des chaussures	 des chaussettes
 une robe	 un chapeau	 un jean

Loto Français – Les vêtements © Colette Elliott and Brilliant Publications. This board may be photocopied for use by the purchaser.

Loto! (Équipe 4)   Nom: _____

 une robe	 un jean	 une chemise
 un short	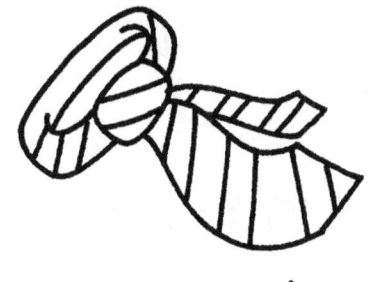 une cravate	 un pull

Loto! (Équipe 1) Nom: _____

un pantalon	une cravate	un pull
un chapeau	une jupe	un jean

Loto Français – Les vêtements

Loto! (Équipe 2) Nom: _____

une jupe	des chaussures	une chemise
un jean	un t-shirt	un pantalon

Loto! (Équipe 3) Nom: _____

un short	des chaussures	des chaussettes
une robe	un chapeau	un jean

Loto Français – Les vêtements

Loto! (Équipe 4) Nom: _____

une robe	un jean	une chemise
un short	une cravate	un pull

Loto Français – Les vêtements

Noël

Team 1 to win	Start on 2 or 7
Team 2 to win	Start on 1, 3, 4 or 12
Team 3 to win	Start on 3, 5, 7, 10 or 11
Team 4 to win	Start on 5, 7, 8 or 9
All teams to win	Start on 6

These numbers refer to the numbers on the left and right of the grid below.

Tick the white boxes in the grid as you call out the words.

				Winning team										
				2	1	2&3	2	3&4	All	1,3,4	4	4	3	3	2	
Order of call	1	le houx	the holly													1
	2	la dinde	the turkey													2
	3	le père noël	Father Christmas													3
	4	le bonhomme de neige	the snowman													4
	5	Joyeux noël!	Happy Christmas!													5
	6	le sapin	the Christmas tree													6
	7	le vingt-cinq décembre	25th December													7
	8	l'étoile	the star													8
	9	les cadeaux	the presents													9
	10	la crèche	the crib													10
	11	la bougie	the candle													11
	12	la bûche de noël	a Christmas log													12
	1	le houx	the holly													1
	2	la dinde	the turkey													2
	3	le père noël	Father Christmas													3
	4	le bonhomme de neige	the snowman													4
	5	Joyeux noël!	Happy Christmas!													5
	6	le sapin	the Christmas tree													6
	7	le vingt-cinq décembre	25th December													7
	8	l'étoile	the star													8
	9	les cadeaux	the presents													9

We have used the definite article (le/la) for the Christmas words (instead of the indefinite article as used for other topics) as it seemed more appropriate. This could provide the stimulus for getting children to practise both forms.

Loto! (Équipe 1)   Nom: _____

Loto Français – Noël ©Colette Elliott and Brilliant Publications. This board may be photocopied for use by the purchaser.

- -

Loto! (Équipe 2)   Nom: _____

Loto Français – Noël © Colette Elliott and Brilliant Publications. This board may be photocopied for use by the purchaser.

Loto! (Équipe 4) Nom: _____

Loto Français – Noël

Loto! (Équipe 4) Nom: _____

Loto Français – Noël

Loto! (Équipe 1)   Nom: _____

le bonhomme de neige	la crèche	la dinde

le 25 décembre	l'étoile	

Loto Français – Noël   © Colette Elliott and Brilliant Publications. This board may be photocopied for use by the purchaser.

Loto! (Équipe 2)   Nom: _____

l'étoile	le houx	les cadeaux

	le sapin	le bonhomme de neige

Loto Français – Noël   © Colette Elliott and Brilliant Publications. This board may be photocopied for use by the purchaser.

Loto! (Équipe 3)   Nom: _____

la bûche de noël	le houx	la bougie

le père noël	le 25 décembre	Joyeux Noël!

Loto Français – Noël

Loto! (Équipe 4)   Nom: _____

le père noël	Joyeux Noël!	les cadeaux

la bûche de noël	la crèche	la dinde

Loto! (Équipe 1)   Nom: _____

la bonhomme de neige	la crèche	la dinde
le 25 décembre	l'étoile	Joyeux noël!

Loto! (Équipe 2)   Nom: _____

l'étoile	le houx	les cadeaux
Joyeux noël!	le sapin	le bonhomme de neige

Loto! (Équipe 3)   Nom: _____

la bûche de noël	le houx	la bougie
le père noël	le 25 décembre	Joyeux noël!

Loto Français – Noël

Loto! (Équipe 4)   Nom: _____

le père noël	Joyeux noël!	les cadeaux
la bûche de noël	la crèche	la dinde

Loto! (Équipe   )   Nom: _____

© Colette Elliott and Brilliant Publications. This board may be photocopied for use by the purchaser.

- -

Loto! (Équipe   )   Nom: _____

© Colette Elliott and Brilliant Publications. This board may be photocopied for use by the purchaser.

List of vocabulary used in the games

Les nombres de 1 à 12

un	1
deux	2
trois	3
quatre	4
cinq	5
six	6
sept	7
huit	8
neuf	9
dix	10
onze	11
douze	12

Les nombres de 1 à 60

sept	7
douze	12
quinze	15
dix-neuf	19
vingt-six	26
trente-quatre	34
trente-cinq	35
quarante et un	41
quarante-deux	42
cinquante	50
cinquante-huit	58
soixante	60

Les animaux

un canard	a duck
un chat	a cat
un cheval	a horse
un chien	a dog
un cochon	a pig
un cochon d'Inde	a Guinea pig
un hamster	a hamster
un lapin	a rabbit
un poisson rouge	a goldfish
une poule	a hen
une souris	a mouse
une vache	a cow

Bon appétit!

des bonbons	(some) sweets
des frites	(some) chips
du fromage	(some) cheese
un gâteau	a cake
une glace	an ice-cream
un œuf	an egg
du pain	(some) bread
un poulet	a chicken
une pomme	an apple
du jambon	(some) ham
une pomme de terre	a potato
du lait	(some) milk

En classe

un bâton de colle	a glue stick
un cahier	an exercise book
une calculatrice	a calculator
un cartable	a school bag
des ciseaux	(some) scissors
un crayon	a pencil
une gomme	a rubber
un livre	a book
une règle	a ruler
un stylo	a pen
un taille-crayon	a pencil sharpener
une trousse	a pencil case

Les vêtements

un chapeau	a hat
des chaussettes	(some) socks
des chaussures	(some) shoes
une chemise	a shirt
une cravate	a tie
un jean	a pair of jeans
une jupe	a skirt
un pantalon	a pair of trousers
un pull	a jumper
une robe	a dress
un short	a pair of shorts
un t-shirt	a T-shirt

Noël

le houx	the holly
la dinde	the turkey
le père noël	Father Christmas
Joyeux noël!	Happy Christmas!
le sapin	the Christmas tree
le 25 décembre	25th December
l'étoile	the star
les cadeaux	the presents
la crèche	the crib
la bougie	the candle
la bûche de noël	the Christmas log (Yule log)
le bonhomme de neige	the snowman

Ages: 7–11yrs

Jouons Tous Ensemble

20 Games to Play with Children to Encourage and Reinforce French Language and Vocabulary

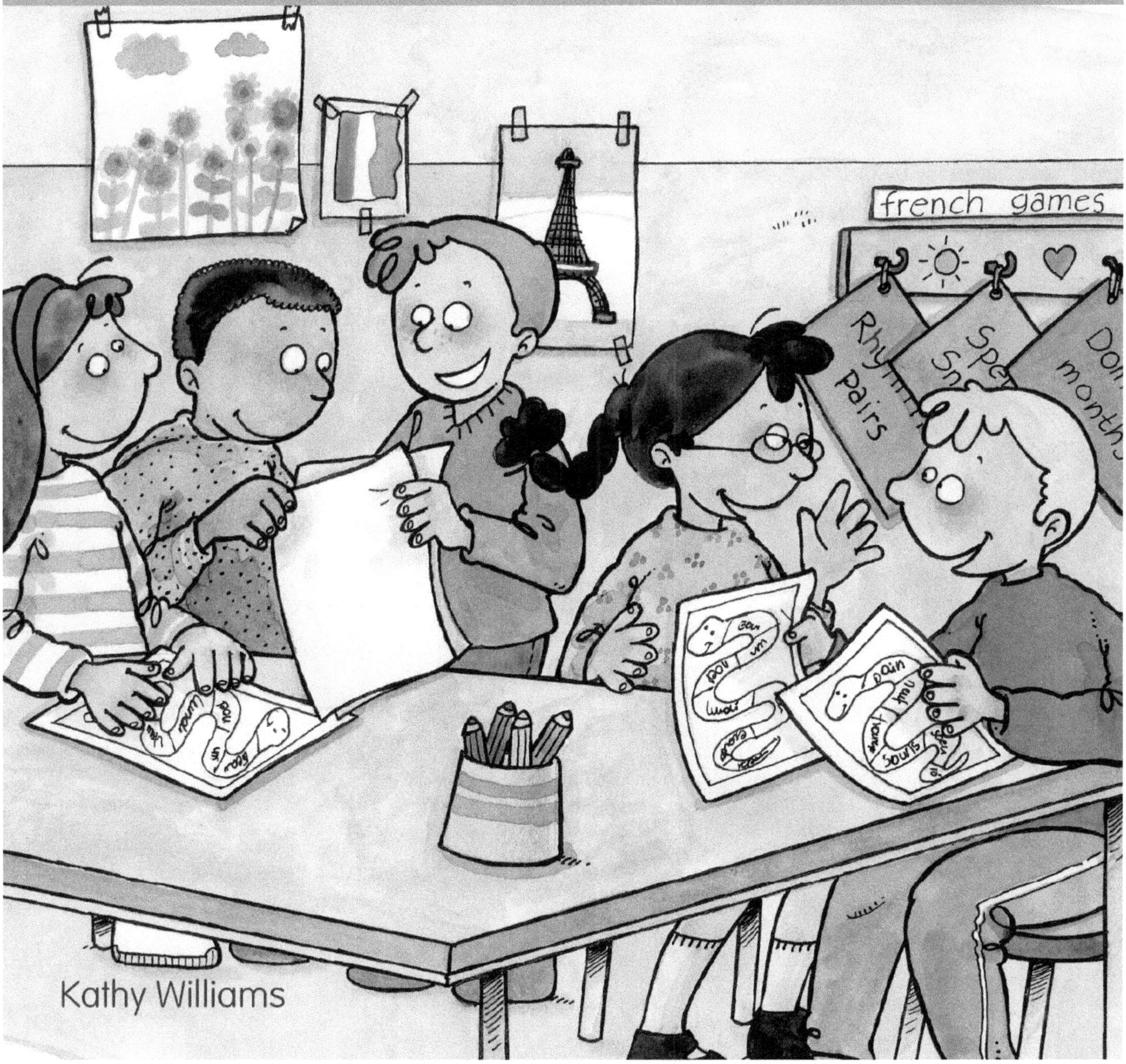

Kathy Williams

Jouons Tous Ensemble

20 Games to Play with Children to Encourage and Reinforce French Language and Vocabulary

Kathy Williams

We hope you and your pupils enjoy playing the games in this book. Brilliant Publications publishes many other books for teaching modern foreign languages. To find out more details on any of the titles listed below, please go to our website: www.brilliantpublications.co.uk.

100+ Fun Ideas for Practising Modern Foreign Languages in the Primary Classroom	978-1-903853-98-6
More Fun Ideas for Advancing Modern Foreign Languages in the Primary Classroom	978-1-905780-72-3
Chantez Plus Fort!	978-1-903853-37-5
Hexagonie 1	978-1-905780-59-4
Hexagonie 2	978-1-905780-18-1
C'est Français!	978-1-903853-02-3
J'aime Chanter!	978-1-905780-11-2
J'aime Parler!	978-1-905780-12-9
French Pen Pals Made Easy	978-1-905780-10-5
Loto Français	978-1-905780-45-7
French Festivals and Traditions	978-1-905780-44-0
Unforgettable French	978-1-78317-093-7
Bonne Idée	978-1-905780-62-4
¡Es Español!	978-1-903853-64-1
Juguemos Todos Juntos	978-1-903853-95-5
¡Vamos a Cantar!	978-1-905780-13-6
Spanish Pen Pals Made Easy	978-1-905780-42-3
Lotto en Español	978-1-905780-47-1
Spanish Festivals and Traditions	978-1-905780-53-2
Buena idea	978-1-905780-63-1
Das ist Deutsch	978-1-905780-15-0
Wir Spielen Zusammen	978-1-903853-97-9
German Pen Pals Made Easy	978-1-905780-43-3
Deutsch-Lotto	978-1-905780-46-4
German Festivals and Traditions	978-1-905780-52-5
Gute Idee	978-1-905780-65-5
Giochiamo Tutti Insieme	978-1-903853-96-2
Lotto in Italiano	978-1-905780-48-8
Buon'Idea	978-0-85747-696-8

Published by Brilliant Publications Limited
Unit 10, Sparrow Hall Farm
Edlesborough
Dunstable
Bedfordshire
LU6 2ES, UK

Website: www.brilliantpublications.co.uk
General information enquiries:
Tel: 01525 222292
E-mail: info@brilliantpublications.co.uk

The name Brilliant Publications and the logo are registered trademarks.

Written by Kathy Williams
Cover and inside illustrations by Chantal Kees
© Kathy Williams 2006

Printed ISBN: 978-1-903853-81-8
epdf ISBN: 978-0-85747-190-1

Printed in the UK.
First published 2006. Reprinted 2007(twice) and 2009.
10 9 8 7 6 5 4

The right of Kathy Williams to be identified as the author of this work has been asserted by her in accordance with the Copyright, Designs and Patents Act 1988.

Pages 10, 12–13, 15–17, 20, 22, 24, 26–28, 30–31, 33–34, 36–37, 39, 41–42, 44, 47–48, 50 and 52 may be photocopied by the purchasing institution or individual teachers for classroom use only, without permission from the publisher and without declaration to the Copyright Licensing Agency or Publishers' Licensing Services. No other part of this book may be reproduced in any other form or for any other purpose, without the prior permission of the publisher.

Contents

All the games involve speaking, and most can be adapted to practise alternative language. See individual game descriptions for ideas.

	Language focus	Page
Introduction		4

Games involving speech and action

Bonjour ball game	introductions	5
Colour relay	colours	6
Slap down numbers	numbers	7
Calling all animals	animals	8

Games particularly involving writing/spelling

Domino months	months	9–10
Write back	numbers	11–13
Rhyming pairs	familiar words	14–17
Spelling snake	any language	18–20
Sort yourself out	familiar words	21–22
Silly sentences	familiar words	23–24

Games involving cards/boards and speech/writing

Wacky meals	food	25–28
House designers	rooms	29–31
Super sporty week	sports/days	32–34
Weather reporters	weather	35–37
Triple time	time	38–39
The best/worst day ever at school	school subjects/time	40–42
Like it or not	likes and dislikes	43–44
A tour of France	transport/places in France	45–48
Quiz corners	any language	49–50
Rock, paper, scissors	any language	51–52

Introduction

The games in this book are designed to complement language teaching and learning, either in the classroom or at home. They are fun to play, and there is no age limit – children and adults alike can enjoy the different types of games.

Each game concentrates on one or two specific language areas. Many of the games can be adapted to practise other language vocabulary as appropriate.

All the games encourage speaking and listening. The skills of reading and writing are emphasized to different degrees in the different games.

The instructions for each game set out:
- the objectives for the game
- how to set it up
- how to play it
- extensions/variations

Some of the games require cards and boards and these are provided as photocopiable resource pages. It is a good idea to allow some time to prepare the items needed for each game before introducing them into play. If the playing cards and boards are photocopied onto thin card and laminated, you will be able to use them again and again for many years.

Bonjour ball game

Action game

Objectives
- To practise key introduction words
- Game can be extended to include other introduction phrases as required

```
Mots clés – Key words
bonjour              hello
au revoir            goodbye
ça va?               how are you?
ça va bien, merci    I'm fine, thank you
je m'appelle …       my name is …
```

Setting up the game
- You need two or more different coloured balls.

How to play the game

1. Pupils stand in two lines facing each other. The end pupil starts with one of the balls, and throws it to the pupil opposite. That person then throws the ball to the pupil diagonally opposite, who throws it this time to the person directly opposite and so on. The ball thus makes its way in a zig-zag along the two lines.

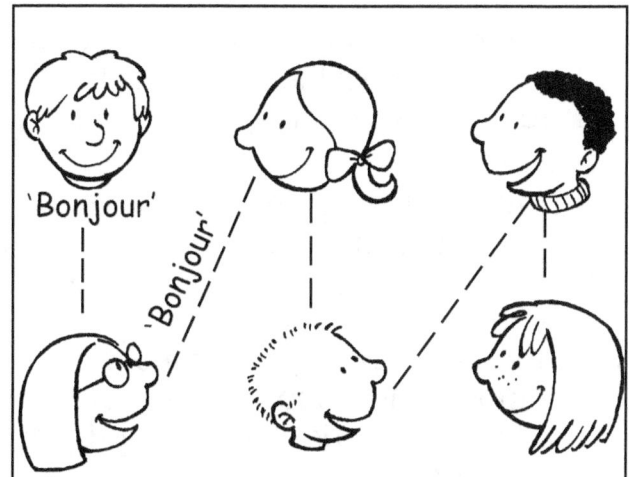

2. While throwing and catching the ball, each pupil must say 'Bonjour'. Using a different coloured ball, repeat the game, but this time say 'Au revoir'.
3. Now, tell the children to take note of the colour of the ball. Using the red ball, for instance, they say 'Bonjour', and with the blue ball, they say 'Au revoir'.
4. Start the game off with one ball again, then introduce the other ball after a couple of throws. This makes them think about which word they are saying! You could introduce further coloured balls with 'Ça va?', 'Ça va bien, merci', 'Je m'appelle …'. Try as many as the group can manage!
5. As a rounding-up test, stand in a large circle, and pick a pupil to hold the coloured balls in the centre. They then throw the balls (gently!) to pupils at random who must say the appropriate phrase for that colour of ball as it is thrown. Younger pupils may find that concentrating on more than two colours/phrases at once is too difficult, but older groups will enjoy the challenge of several colours/phrases in this game.

Extensions/variations
- Adapt the game to practise vocabulary groups; each time a player catches the ball the pupil must say a different animal word/colour/food item.
- Use the ball throwing idea to practise lists of words, passing the ball up and down the line or in a circle; practise the alphabet in French/days/months/numbers.

Colour relay

Action game

Objective
- To practise saying colour words and respond by picking up the correct colour from a choice

Setting up the game
- Pupils play in teams.
- You will need several items of different colours, the same number of items for each team.
- The game is best played in a large space so that the participants can run back and forth.

Mots clés – Key words
rouge	red
blanc	white
bleu	blue
noir	black
vert	green
rose	pink
jaune	yellow
marron	brown
orange	orange
gris	grey

How to play the game
1. Place sets of coloured items in piles at one end of the room (or space you are playing in).
2. The teams line up opposite the coloured items so that they can race against each other in a back-and-forth relay.
3. The teacher calls out the first colour to start the race.
4. The first team member from each team runs to collect that coloured item from their team pile, and returns to the team.
5. On their return they say another colour (in French) to be picked up. The next player runs to collect that coloured item, returns to the rest of the team and says the next colour to be picked up.
6. The game continues in this way, with players joining the back of the line on their return to the team, storing all the items at the back of the line, until all the coloured items have been collected.
7. The winning team is the one that successfully collects all the items first. It is a good idea to have three or four small teams, with extra helpers to monitor the teams, so that everyone gets more than one turn, and you can listen carefully to the players saying the colours in FRENCH. You could have a rule that anyone heard saying the wrong colour, or not using French, has to run back and forth again (without picking up another item) before the next player has a turn.

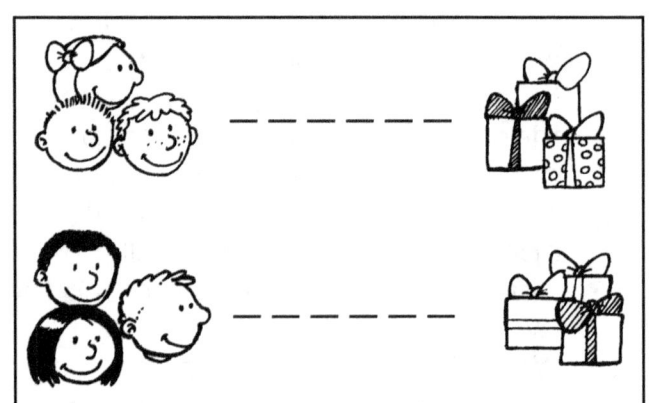

Extension/variation
- To make the game more challenging pupils could say two or three colours at once, with plenty of items in the pile to choose from.

Jouons Tous Ensemble © Kathy Williams

Slap down numbers

Action game

Objectives
- To practise saying the numbers one to ten
- To listen carefully
- To respond quickly to recognition of numbers in French

Mots clés – Key words

un	one
deux	two
trois	three
quatre	four
cinq	five
six	six
sept	seven
huit	eight
neuf	nine
dix	ten

Setting up the game
- Players are in pairs, sitting at a table, or where they can put their hands down quickly onto a flat surface.

How to play the game
1. Toss a coin to decide who starts. Both players have their hands on their heads to begin the game.
2. Choose one player to start first. Both players count together in French, slowly.
3. When the counting reaches the number that player one has decided to stop at, he slaps his hands down, and spreads out the appropriate number of fingers on the table. For example the counting goes: 'un … deux … trois …' but on 'quatre' he slaps his hand down showing four fingers. Encourage the children to use both hands.
4. Player two must respond as quickly as possible by putting her hands down too, BUT she too must only put down the correct number of fingers, i.e. in this case only four.
5. If she puts the correct number of fingers down, then she becomes the caller. If she is not correct then player one continues to make the number choices.

Extension/variation
- The game can be made more challenging by counting up in twos, by counting backwards or by counting very quickly.

© Kathy Williams   *Jouons Tous Ensemble*

Calling all animals

Action game

Objective
- To practise saying animal words

Mots clés – Key words
chat (m)	cat
souris (f)	mouse
chien (m)	dog
araignée (f)	spider
cheval (m)	horse
grenouille (f)	frog
lapin (m)	rabbit
poisson (m)	fish
oiseau (m)	bird
cochon d'Inde (m)	guinea-pig

Setting up the game
- Any number of pupils can play. Each player can have a different animal name given to them if there are 10 or less players; if there are more players the animal words can be used more than once.
- You need enough space for the group to form a circle.

How to play the game
1. The group forms a circle and one pupil is chosen at random to be 'it', in the middle of the circle.
2. All the animal words should be introduced and practised first so that everyone is familiar with the words.
3. Each player is then given an animal name. The whole group hears the names being given out and they can all practise each word as it is introduced. Make sure that everyone knows exactly how to say what they are, and that the person in the middle can say all the animal words (some reminding might be needed).
4. The player who is 'it' decides on an animal name to say and says it aloud three times in succession.
5. The aim of the game is for the person who has been given that animal name to join in and say their name once but before the 'it' person has finished saying it three times! If the 'animal' succeeds, he/she is then 'it' instead. If the 'it' person manages to say the word three times before the person with that animal name has said his name once, the player in the middle stays as 'it'. Everyone who manages to be 'it' must aim to stay there as long as possible, and all the others must try to get him/her out.
6. If the circle players cannot join in before their names are said three times, adjust to saying the name five times (sometimes needed for younger children).

Extensions/variations
- This game is very adaptable as it can be played with any vocabulary that you wish to practise, e.g. buildings, food, parts of the body. It works well with French girls'/boys' names.
- Another way to play is for you to spell the animal word out, either in French or English. The player who thinks that the animal name is theirs has to run around the outside of the circle back to their place before you finish spelling the word (do it slowly to give them a chance!), and say the word to make sure they were right to run.

Jouons Tous Ensemble © Kathy Williams

Domino months

Spelling game

Objective
- To practise the months in French with particular emphasis on word recognition in writing

Setting up the game
- Pupils can either play in pairs or groups with one set of dominoes (page 10) per pair.
- The dominoes could be coloured, decorated, and laminated and/or mounted on card before use.

Mots clés – Key words
janvier	January
février	February
mars	March
avril	April
mai	May
juin	June
juillet	July
août	August
septembre	September
octobre	October
novembre	November
décembre	December

How to play the game
1. Place the dominoes face down in front of the players with one domino upturned to start the game. The aim of the game is to match the dominoes to make complete month words.
2. Players each take five dominoes at random and look at them without revealing them to their opponent(s). The rest of the dominoes are put in a pile on the table.
3. One player takes a turn first, trying to complete a month word by placing one of his dominoes before or after the starting domino. Dominoes can be placed at right angles so the words do not have to go in one continuous straight line. If the first player cannot go, the other player(s) take their turn. If none of the players can place a domino, then the first player picks one up from the pile and plays the card if it completes a domino month. Play continues with players either putting down a domino or picking one up from the pile.
4. The winner is the player who uses up all of their dominoes first, or who has the least number of cards left. It isn't always possible to carry on until all the dominoes have been put down. In the case of a tie-break, maybe add the number of letters on each card together, the person with the least being the winner!
5. You will need to monitor correct positioning of the dominoes to ensure correct word completion. Saying the names of the months out loud as they are completed helps to link the written and spoken words.

© Kathy Williams   *Jouons Tous Ensemble*

Domino months

Enlarge photocopy at 115% onto thin card and cut out.

obre	nov	embre	jui	embre	ju
embre	déc	llet	oct	vier	sept
obre	av	ril	ma	in	fév
rier	ma	i	ju	ût	jan
vier	fév	in	oct	vier	jui
rs	jan	rs	jan	ût	ma
rier	ao	llet	ao	llet	jui

This page may be photocopied for use by the purchasing institution only.

Jouons Tous Ensemble

Write back

Spelling game

Objectives
- To reinforce knowledge of numbers up to twenty
- Version 1 practises recognition of number words. Version 2 reinforces the spellings of the numbers

Setting up the game
- Pupils play in pairs using one of the grids from number sheet (page 12) per pair, or one customized in advance to practise specific numbers or words (page 13).
- The children will need some counters or coins.

How to play the game

Version 1
1. The players have a number grid in front of them. Depending on their skill, this can be either A, B or C (from page 12) or one you have custom made using page 13.
2. Player one looks at the grid, decides on a number, but does not tell their partner. Using a finger, player one gently taps out that amount on their partner's back.
3. The partner then places a counter on the correct number on the grid and recites the number in French.
4. The game continues with each player taking turns until all the numbers are covered.

Version 2
1. The players have a grid as in version 1, but instead of tapping the required number of times for their partner to recognize, they must slowly spell out the word on their partner's back. It is best to 'draw' one letter at a time, rather than write the whole word in joined-up writing. However, the whole word technique can work with older or more able pupils.
2. As before, the player on whose back the word is written must place their counter on the correct word on the grid, saying it in French.

Extension/variation
- This game can be adapted to reinforce spellings in any language area using the blank grid to set out the language to be practised. Alternatively, the 'receiving' player writes down what they think has been spelled on their back onto a blank grid.

Mots clés – Key words

un	one
deux	two
trois	three
quatre	four
cinq	five
six	six
sept	seven
huit	eight
neuf	nine
dix	ten
onze	eleven
douze	twelve
treize	thirteen
quatorze	fourteen
quinze	fifteen
seize	sixteen
dix-sept	seventeen
dix-huit	eighteen
dix-neuf	nineteen
vingt	twenty

Write back number grid

Photocopy one grid per pair (can use either Grid A, B or C)

Grid A

un	deux	trois	quatre	cinq
six	sept	huit	neuf	dix

Grid B

un	deux	trois	quatre	cinq
six	sept	huit	neuf	dix
onze	douze	treize	quatorze	quinze
seize	dix-sept	dix-huit	dix-neuf	vingt

Grid C

onze	douze	treize	quatorze	quinze
seize	dix-sept	dix-huit	dix-neuf	vingt

This page may be photocopied for use by the purchasing institution only.

Jouons Tous Ensemble © Kathy Williams

Write back blank number grid

Use this to prepare the language that you want to practise, or use the grid to write your answers in.

Grid A

Grid B

Grid C

Rhyming pairs

Spelling game

Objectives
- To facilitate close examination of familiar words in their written form
- To introduce the concept of using word endings to help identify word gender (all the words used are masculine, with the obvious exception of **mère**)
- Saying the words out loud links the spelling patterns with pronunciation and helps pupils to distinguish between similar sounding, but differently spelled word endings

Mots clés – Key words
pantal**on**	trousers
cray**on**	pencil
franç**ais**	French
angl**ais**	English
p**ain**	bread
cop**ain**	friend
caf**é**	coffee
supermarch**é**	supermarket
bat**eau**	boat
ois**eau**	bird
m**ère** (f)	mother
p**ère**	father
chev**eux**	hair
y**eux**	eyes
lap**in**	rabbit
jard**in**	garden
cah**ier**	exercise book
gren**ier**	attic

Setting up the game
- You need to photocopy and cut out the rhyme cards (pages 15–16).
- The children will need some counters or coins.
- Players play in groups of three. Each pupil will need to pick a picture board from the selection (pages 16–17).

How to play the game
1. All the cards are placed face down and spread out on the table in front of the players.
2. The game is played as a matching pictures pairs game, only this time the matching pairs are rhyming written words.
3. Players must take turns to turn over two cards at random.
4. If they have a rhyming pair they say the two words.
5. If the pair does not rhyme they turn the cards back over and try to remember for next time where each card is.
6. When a player finds a matching pair he/she looks to see if the pair is pictured on their board.
7. If it is, they place counters or coins on the appropriate pictures and put the cards to one side. If the cards aren't pictured, he/she puts them back in the middle of the table, face down.
8. The winner is the player who completes their board first.

Extension/variation
- Players could play the game using boards and words they have created themselves. They could use vocabulary they already know (chosen either individually or as a group) or use dictionaries to look up new words.

Rhyming pairs game cards

pantalon	crayon
français	anglais
pain	copain
café	supermarché
mère	père
bateau	oiseau

Rhyming pairs game cards

lapin	jardin
cheveux	yeux
cahier	grenier

This page may be photocopied for use by the purchasing institution only.

Rhyming pairs board

Spelling snake

Spelling game

Objective
- To encourage the use of a specific area of vocabulary or to give players the opportunity to use any language that they know

Setting up the game
- This game can be played with four or more people.
- Each child needs a blank copy of the 'spelling snake' (page 20).

How to play the game
1. Start as a whole group and brainstorm a large number of words within a vocabulary area, or several areas. At the end of this session, write these words, correctly spelled onto the board, or provide a prepared list that contains the words you elicited from the players. (This list would benefit from containing words that start or finish with a variety of letters – take care that not all your words end in the letter 'e' for example).
2. Give the players a couple of minutes to study the words, then remove them from view.
3. Each player writes one word of their choice from the target list into the first section of their 'spelling snake' (see 'Commence ici').
4. All players then simultaneously pass the snake on to another player, and here you must ensure random exchanges.
5. Using the final letter of the first word, each player must then write in a new word from the list, and then pass the snake on as before.
6. If a player cannot write a word starting with the last letter (which is often not possible), he/she writes a new word that is unconnected and passes on the snake as before.
7. The class continue to write on and pass around the snakes until all the spaces are full. You can make the game easier by allowing repeats of the same word, or harder by having a 'no repeats' rule.
8. When the snakes are complete, and there may be some which take longer than others, the snake that each player ends with becomes the one which will score or lose them points.

Jouons Tous Ensemble © Kathy Williams

To score points

- Ask each player to check the words on his snake against the original list. A correctly spelled word gets 2 points. Add on an extra 1 point for every word that starts with the last letter of the previous one. The winner is the player with the highest total of points at the end.
- If you tell the players how the scoring works before they start to play it will encourage everyone to spell correctly as they do not know which snake they will have at the end.

Extensions/variations

- Alternatively, tell the players that they are going to be able to use any words they like during the game, but that spelling must be correct. In this case play the game and then include a follow-up session to go over the words and their spellings together.
- If players do not have time to study the words immediately before the game, this game can be used to test spelling knowledge of a preset group of words.

Spelling snake

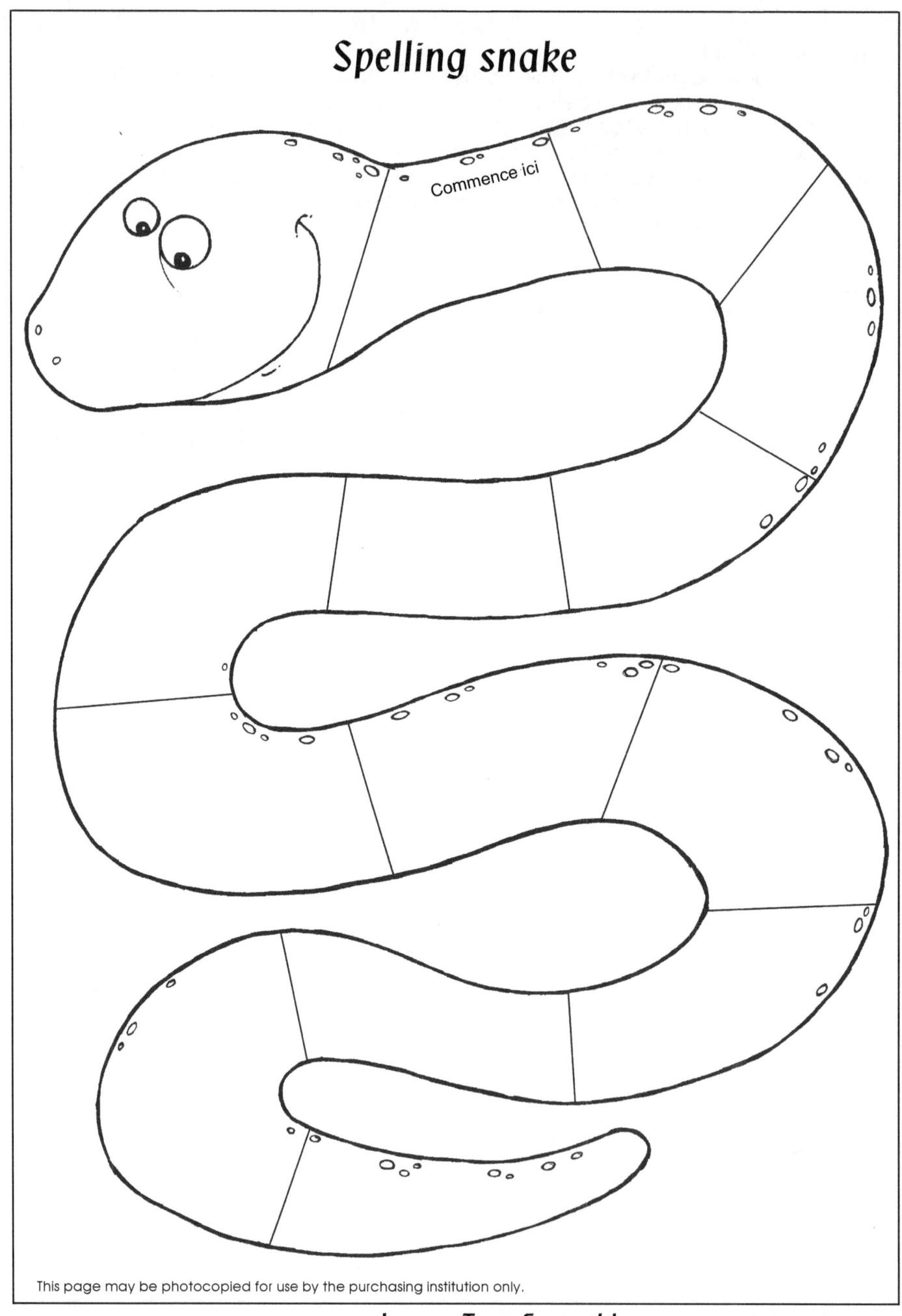

Commence ici

This page may be photocopied for use by the purchasing institution only.

Jouons Tous Ensemble © Kathy Williams

Sort yourself out

Spelling game

Objective
- To arrange sets of words beginning with the same letter into alphabetical order

Setting up the game
- You need 'sort yourself out' list of words (page 22) and blank sheets for the children's answers.
- Children will need some scissors and some pens/pencils.
- Children play in pairs.

How to play the game
1. Cut the word lists into separate columns and give each pair of children one list.
2. The children cut the words out individually into strips and mix them up.
3. They then must try to put their words into alphabetical order. They write down the words and their meanings, guessing for those they don't know. You could set a time limit for this task.
4. At the end of the allotted time, the teacher reads out or writes down the correct alphabetical order for each list and the word meanings. Players get a point for every correct position in the list and a point for each correct meaning.

Extension/variation
- The game can be played again using a different set of words or you could create your own list. This game is very useful for checking the pupils' understanding of vocabulary practised.

Mots clés – Key words

abeille (f)	bee
abricot (m)	apricot
araignée (f)	spider
armoire (f)	cupboard
avion (m)	aeroplane
avril	April
carotte (f)	carrot
cerises (f)	cherries
chapeau (m)	hat
cheval (m)	horse
cheveux (m)	hair
croissant (m)	croissant
garage (m)	garage
genou (m)	knee
gomme (f)	eraser/rubber
grand	big
grenier (m)	attic
gris	grey
lait (m)	milk
lapin (m)	rabbit
lettre (f)	letter
livre (m)	book
lundi (m)	Monday
lune (f)	moon
main (f)	hand
mardi (m)	Tuesday
montagne (f)	mountain
monument (m)	monument
musée (m)	museum
musique (f)	music
rectangle (m)	rectangle
règle (f)	ruler
reine (f)	queen
rideau (m)	curtain
riz (m)	rice
rose (f)	rose, pink
salle à manger (f)	dining room
salon (m)	lounge
sandwich (m)	sandwich
sœur (f)	sister
souris (f)	mouse
stylo (m)	pen
tapis (m)	rug
talon (m)	claw
thé (m)	tea
train (m)	train
treize	thirteen
trousse (f)	pencil case
vendredi (m)	Friday
ver (m)	worm
verre (f)	glass
violon (m)	violin
voiture (f)	car
volcan (m)	volcano

© Kathy Williams *Jouons Tous Ensemble*

Sort yourself out

abeille	carotte	garage
abricot	cerises	genou
araignée	chapeau	gomme
armoire	cheval	grand
avion	cheveux	grenier
avril	croissant	gris
lait	main	rectangle
lapin	mardi	règle
lettre	montagne	reine
livre	monument	rideau
lundi	musée	riz
lune	musique	rose
salle à manger	tapis	vendredi
salon	talon	ver
sandwich	thé	verre
sœur	train	violon
souris	treize	voiture
stylo	trousse	volcan

Silly sentences

Spelling game

Objective
- To encourage recognition of sentence building rules and parts of speech

Setting up the game
- Prepare the game by photocopying and cutting out the word sections (page 24), one for every player or pair of players.

Mots clés – Key words
le fermier	the farmer
le chien	the dog
le chat	the cat
porter	to wear
manger	to eat
chasser	to chase
un chapeau	a hat
un saucisson	a sausage
un ballon	a balloon
délicieux	delicious
long	long
rouge	red
vert	green
bleu	blue

How to play the game
1. Give each player (or pair) a set of mixed-up word sections.
2. Discuss the parts of a sentence: noun (le nom), verb (le verbe), adjective (l'adjectif – m). Point out that in French the adjective usually follows the noun. (There are some exceptions to this rule: some commonly used adjectives come before the noun but none are used here).
3. Demonstrate a sentence that makes sense, for example 'Le fermier porte un chapeau rouge'.
4. Ask the players to form as many sensible sentences as they can, by changing around the words. Look at and discuss the parts of speech and word order.
5. Ask the pupils to see what 'silly' sentences they can create. Remember that the 'silly' sentences should still be formed correctly, ie, 'Le chien mange un chapeau délicieux'.

Extensions/variations
- You could add a selection of adjectives that always precede the noun, such as 'petit (small), grand (big), vieux (old), beau (beautiful)', to reinforce the different positions of adjectives when building sentences.
- Players could draw pictures of their favourite sentences. Play a mime game, where a pupil has to mime what has been drawn and the other players have to guess the 'silly' sentence.

© Kathy Williams   *Jouons Tous Ensemble*

Silly sentences

| le fermier | porte | un chapeau | rouge | et vert |

| le chien | mange | un saucisson | délicieux |

| le chat | chasse | un ballon | long | et bleu |

Jouons Tous Ensemble

Wacky meals

Card game

Objective
- To recognize and use some food words, as well as the correct words for the different meal times

Setting up the game
- Players are in pairs or small groups.
- Each group will need a set of food word cards (page 27) and a 'menu' (page 28).

How to play the game
1. Each group has a set of food cards face down in front of them.
2. One player picks up a card at random and places it face up in the first 'petit-déjeuner' position on the menu, saying aloud what the food item is in French.
3. The second player then picks up another card and places it on the next breakfast position, saying the food item in French. Some strange breakfast choices may be beginning to appear!
4. Players continue until all the meals are set.
5. When finished they discuss together what meals have been created using the sentence structures: 'Pour le petit-déjeuner je prends ….' And so on.
6. Each pair or group then presents the 'wacky meals' that they have on their menus to the rest of the class.

Mots clés – Key words

pour …	for …
le déjeuner	lunch
le petit-déjeuner	breakfast
le diner/souper	dinner/supper
je prends …	I'm having …
une pomme	an apple
du pain	some bread
du beurre	some butter
un gateau	a cake
des carottes	some carrots
du fromage	some cheese
du chocolat	some chocolate
des pommes de terre	some potatoes
des petits-pois	some peas
des chips	some crisps
un croissant	a croissant
un hot-dog	a hot dog
du coca	some cola
un sandwich	a sandwich
du jambon	some ham
un thé	a tea
une eau minérale	a mineral water
des frites	some chips

Extensions/variations
- The picture cards (page 26) can be used instead of the food word cards to prompt usage of food words.
- The game can be played as a whole class if the menu sheet is enlarged. Individuals take turns to choose cards and place them or write the food item onto the menu.
- Using the same concept, make cards showing different items of clothing, and instead of a menu sheet, use places/events to dress for, for example 'Pour aller **en vacances** je porte … (To go **on holiday** I wear …); Pour aller **à l'école** je porte … (To go **to school** I wear …); Pour aller **une boum** je porte …(To go **to a party** I wear …). See what funny outfits emerge!

Wacky meals picture cards

Wacky meals food word cards

une pomme	du pain	du beurre
un gateau	des carottes	du fromage
du chocolat	des pommes de terre	des petits-pois
des chips	un croissant	un hot-dog
du coca	un sandwich	du jambon
un thé	une eau minérale	des frites

Wacky meals menu sheet

Menu choices

1 Pour le petit-déjeuner	2	3
1 Pour le déjeuner	2	3
1 Pour le diner	2	3

This page may be photocopied for use by the purchasing institution only.

Jouons Tous Ensemble © Kathy Williams

House designers

Board/card game

Objectives
- To use the names for rooms in the house
- To communicate information about the layout of a house
- The use of 'ici' (here) and 'là' (there) and 'c'est' (this/it is) can also be reinforced

Mots clés – Key words
ici	here
là	there
c'est	it is/this is
est	is
la cuisine	the kitchen
le salon	the lounge
la chambre	the bedroom
le vestibule	the hall
la salle de bains	the bathroom
le garage	the garage
la salle à manger	the dining room
le grenier	the attic

Setting up the game
- Pupils play in teams of three, with the teams racing each other.
- Two 'house design sheets' (page 30) are needed per group. Room pictures (page 31) can be used for guidance.
- A spacious room/area (two rooms could be used) to separate two of the three players in each team, so that they cannot see the other player's sheet.

How to play the game
1. One pair of players (players two and three) has a 'house design sheet', a set of room pictures, and a pen/pencil, and sits some distance away from their other team-mate, or in another room.
2. Player one in the team has a 'house design sheet' and a pen/pencil.
3. Player one starts the game by deciding which room to designate first. For example, if he/she decides that the upstairs room on the right is the bedroom, he/she writes 'la chambre' or draws a picture of a bed inside that room.
4. When all the player ones from each competing team have made their decision the teacher tells the player twos to start.
5. Player two from each team visits his/her team-mate to find out which room has been chosen, while player three remains behind with a blank 'house design sheet'. On his return, player two tells player three what and where the room is on their design sheet, **in French, not in English!** For example, in this case, they will need to point to the upstairs right room 'ici' and say 'c'est la chambre'. Player three must then write in the words 'la chambre', or draw an appropriate picture, in the correct room.
6. In the meantime player one chooses another room. Player two returns to player one to find out the whereabouts of the next room and returns to player three to relay that piece of information.
7. The winning team is the one who is first in relaying all the information correctly. Remind players that all of the information should be spoken in French, and although a picture may be drawn instead, this will only take up extra time.

© Kathy Williams   *Jouons Tous Ensemble*

House design sheet

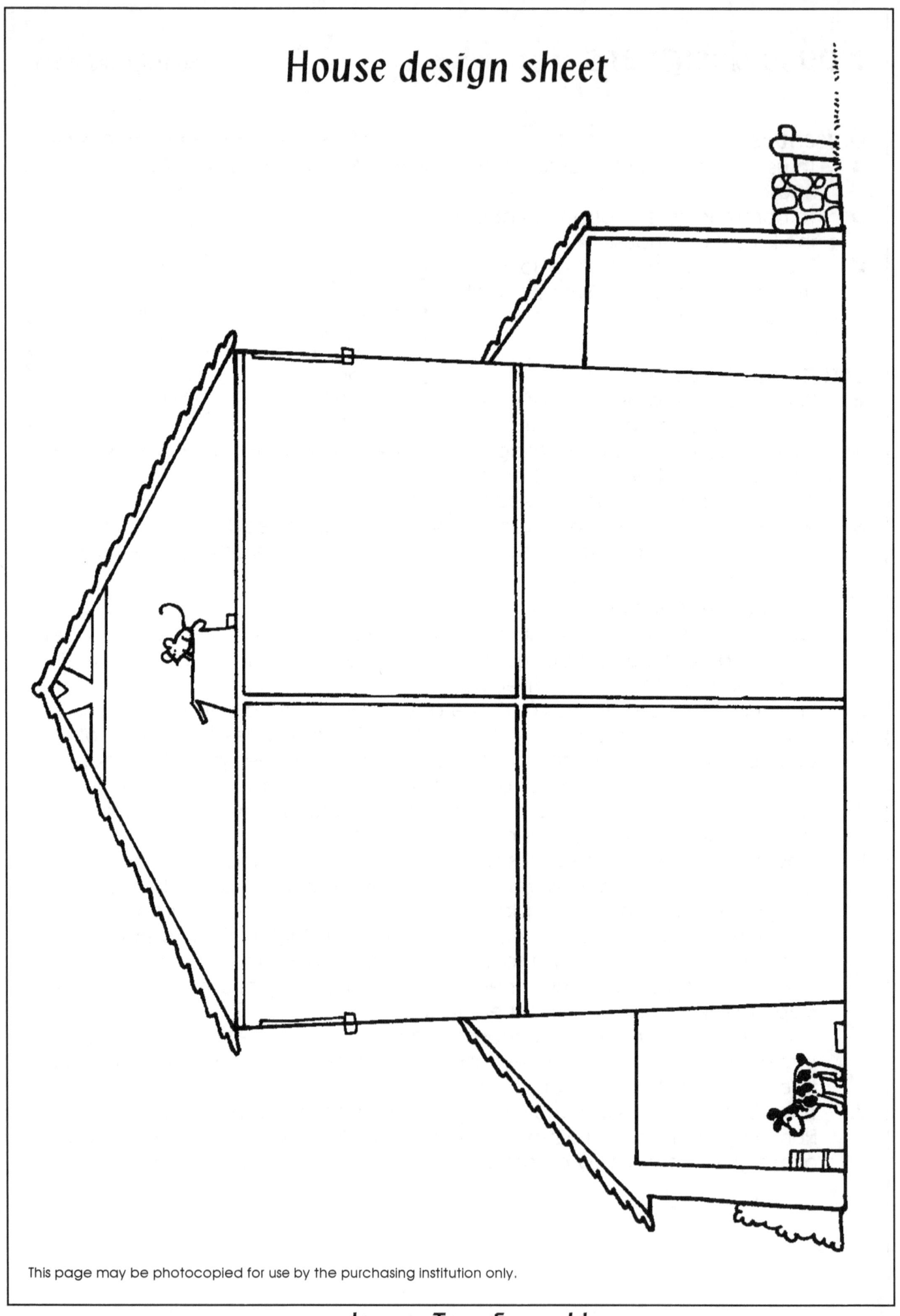

This page may be photocopied for use by the purchasing institution only.

Jouons Tous Ensemble

House designers room pictures

Super sporty week

Board game

Objectives
- To prompt pupils to use the phrases 'je fais ...' and 'je joue ...' in conjunction with seven sport activities
- To practise the days of the week (extension activity)

Setting up the game
- Play in pairs or small groups with one game board (page 33) per group.
- Dice and counters are required.
- Each pupil will need a week planner (page 34).

How to play the game
1. Starting at 'Commence ici' one pupil throws the die and moves the counter the relevant number of places around the board. They must **say** the phrase indicated by the activity picture on the place where they land. They then write the activity onto a day of their choice on the week planner. The next pupil then takes a turn and so on.
2. Pupils continue to throw the die in turn and move repeatedly around the board, until they have landed on **all** the activities and chosen which day to write them in. When they land on activities already used they must still say the appropriate sentence.

Extensions/variations
- You could make the game competitive by having a time limit, or by having the first player to complete their week as the winner. If you wish all pupils to complete the week plan, encourage those who have finished quickly to listen to and help the others, until all have finished.
- As a follow-up activity pupils could present their weekly activity plans to each other or the class, using for example: 'Lundi je fais de l'athlétisme. Mardi je joue au football.' etc.

Mot clés – Key words

je fais ...	I do/go ...
du cyclisme	cycling
de l'athlétisme	athletics
de la natation	swimming
je joue ...	I play ...
au football	football
au rugby	rugby
au basket	basketball
au tennis	tennis
lundi	Monday
mardi	Tuesday
mercredi	Wednesday
jeudi	Thursday
vendredi	Friday
samedi	Saturday
dimanche	Sunday

Jouons Tous Ensemble © Kathy Williams

Super sporty week board game

Commence ici ➡

This page may be photocopied for use by the purchasing institution only.

© Kathy Williams   Jouons Tous Ensemble

Super sporty week board game

lundi	
mardi	
mercredi	
jeudi	
vendredi	
samedi	
dimanche	

This page may be photocopied for use by the purchasing institution only.

Jouons Tous Ensemble

Weather reporters

Board/card game

Objectives
- To ask and answer questions about the weather
- To reinforce the names of some principal towns in France

Setting up the game
- Pupils play together in pairs with one weather grid (page 36) each and a set of town and weather cards (page 37) per pair.

Mots clés – Key words
il fait du soleil	it is sunny
il fait du vent	it is windy
il fait mauvais	the weather is bad
il fait beau	it is fine
il fait chaud	it is hot
il fait froid	it is cold
il pleut	it is raining
il neige	it is snowing
quel temps fait-il?	what's the weather like?
à	at/in

How to play the game
1. Put the town cards and the weather cards in two piles, face down.
2. Using the weather grids, both players first make a weather prediction for each of their towns and tell them to their partner in French. They record their forecasts in writing or by drawing a picture in the 'weather forecast' column on the grid.
3. One player then picks up a town name card and asks what the weather is like there using 'Quel temps fait-il à …?' e.g. 'Quel temps fait-il à Nice?' The town card used is put to one side.
4. The other player picks a weather card and answers using the weather pictured, e.g. 'À Nice il pleut'. The cards can be interpreted in a number of possible ways, for example the sun card could be 'Il fait beau / Il fait du soleil / Il fait chaud.' If this is what either player predicted they put a tick in the second column; if they were wrong they put a cross. The weather card used is returned to the bottom of the pile.
5. The players swap roles and continue asking and answering until all the towns' weather conditions have been filled in on the grid.
6. The winner is the player who scored the most ticks at the end of the game.

Jouons Tous Ensemble

Weather reporters town grid

Town	Weather forecast	✓ or ✗
Paris		
Nice		
Marseille		
Bordeaux		
Lyon		
Toulouse		
Strasbourg		
Calais		

Weather reports

Paris	Lyon	Marseille	Toulouse
Nice	Bordeaux	Calais	Strasbourg

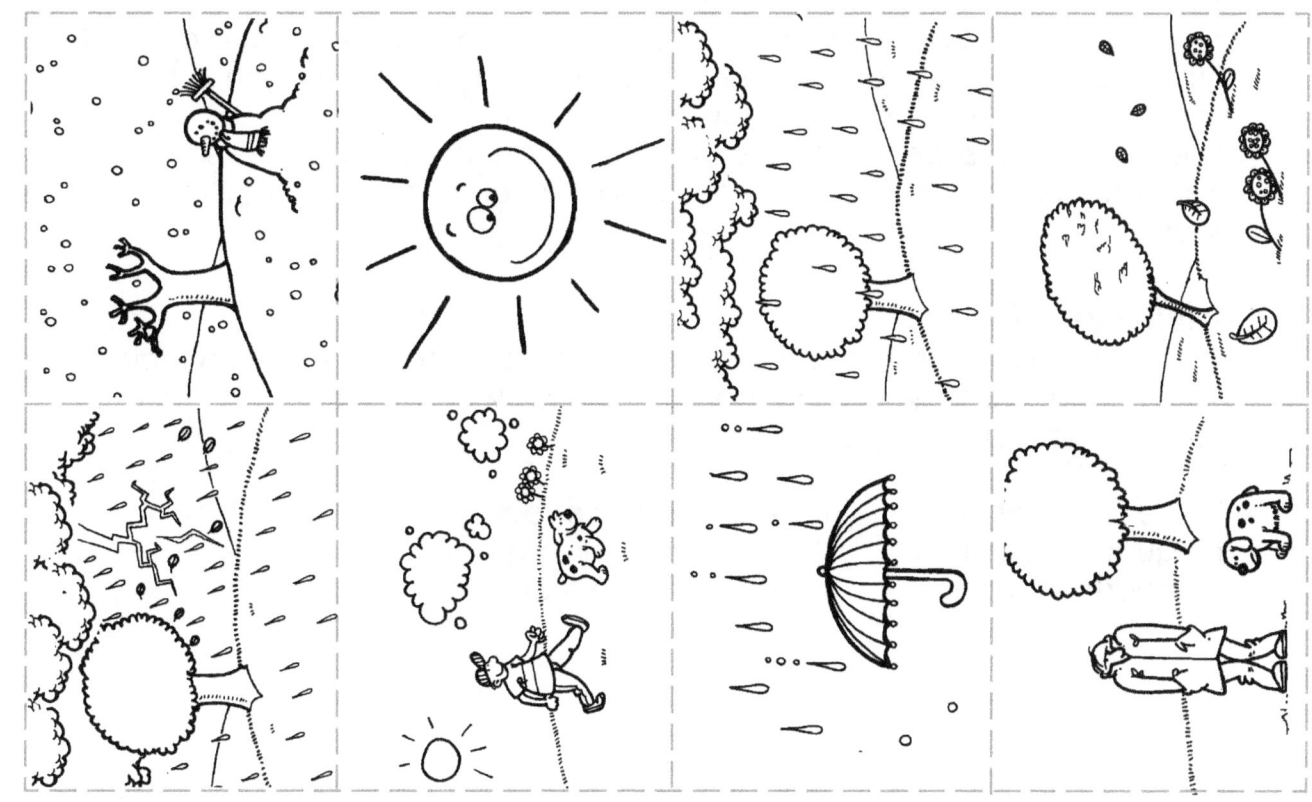

This page may be photocopied for use by the purchasing institution only.

Jouons Tous Ensemble

Triple time

Card game

Objectives
- To practise telling the time in French
- To reinforce understanding of digital and analogue times and the times written out in French

Setting up the game
- Pupils work in pairs.
- Pupils need one set of time cards from page 39 per pair. You could make more cards to practise other times.

> **Mots clés – Key words**
> il est …   it is …
> une heure   one o'clock
> deux heures   two o'clock
> trois heures   three o'clock
> quatre heures   four o'clock
> cinq heures   five o'clock
> six heures   six o'clock
> sept heures   seven o'clock
> huit heures   eight o'clock
> neuf heures   nine o'clock
> dix heures   ten o'clock
> onze heures   eleven o'clock
> midi   midday
> minuit   midnight

How to play the game
1. In pairs, players have a set of time cards in front of them, face down on the table.
2. One player turns over three different cards, trying to find a matching set of three. If he finds three which all say the same time – in digital, analogue and in French – he keeps the set. If the three cards do not match, they are turned face down again and the other player has a turn. (The game works just like a 'pairs' game, except that the players are finding three cards.)
3. To aid the players' chances of finding a match, if they turn over two which match in one go, they keep these to one side until their next turn, when they have three chances to find the third card. If the third card is not found during that turn, they keep the pair to the side until the third is found on a further turn. If their opponent turns over the card that they are missing from their set, this card must be returned to the table, face down.
4. When the players are turning over the cards, encourage them to say the times out loud in French every time, using a whole sentence, e.g. 'Il est cinq heures.'

Extension/variation
- The times are only on the hour, so that players can concentrate on their French. You could make more cards which show half past, quarter to, etc if you feel that your pupils can manage.

    It is half past ten.   It est dix heures et demie.
    It is quarter past three.   It est trois heures et quart.
    It is quarter to one.   It est une heure moins le quart.

Triple time cards

Set 1

Il est trois heures.	3:00	
Il est neuf heures.	9:00	
Il est onze heures.	11:00	
Il est midi/minuit.	12:00	

Set 2

Il est huit heures.	8:00	
Il est quatre heures.	4:00	
Il est deux heures.	2:00	
Il est six heures.	6:00	

This page may be photocopied for use by the purchasing institution only.

© Kathy Williams   Jouons Tous Ensemble

www.brilliantpublications.co.uk

The best/worst day ever at school
Grid game

Objectives
- To practise saying school subjects
- To practise counting
- To practise saying times on the hour

Setting up the game
- Pupils need a 'school day timetable' (page 41) each and one 'Chinese counter' per pair (page 42). Cut out the grid and fold to make the counter.
- Pupils work in pairs.

How to play the game
1. Players fill in their 'ideal' timetable first in the right-hand column of the school day timetable sheet. They then fold back this column so that they cannot see the subjects they have written.
2. Player one picks a time for a lesson from his/her timetable at random, e.g. 'trois heures'.
3. Player two (who has the 'Chinese counter') counts and moves the counter in and out **three** times, counting 'un, deux, trois'.
4. Player one then picks one of the numbers visible on the counter, in French e.g. if five is visible he/she may pick that and say 'cinq'.
5. Player two counts and moves the counter again, this time **five** times.
6. Player one then chooses one of the visible numbers on the counter and this time player two lifts up the corresponding flap.
7. Under the flap is a school subject. Player one reads this out to player two, who then writes this into his/her timetable, in the hour that he/she originally chose (in this case 'trois heures'). Players must say out loud the time and subject as they fill this part in, e.g. 'À trois heures j'ai français'.
8. The players keep swapping over roles of choosing and counting so that both players can complete their timetables.
9. When all timetables are complete the class reveal and discuss their results. The best or worst school day!

Extension/variation
- The 'Chinese counter' is a very adaptable resource that can be used for counting practise as well as having different vocabulary written inside. For example, instead of school subjects, write in buildings. The day's timetable can be filled in to say the time that each building is visited on a tour of the town. Use 'je visite …' instead of 'j'ai …'

Mots clés – Key words
(le) français	French
(le) dessin	art
(l') anglais	English
(l') histoire-géo	humanities
(la) musique	music
(l') informatique	ICT
(les) mathématiques	maths
(les) sciences	science
j'ai	I have
un	one
une heure	one o'clock
deux (heures)	two (o'clock)
trois	three
quatre	four
cinq	five
six	six
sept	seven
huit	eight
neuf	nine
dix	ten
onze	eleven
douze	twelve
à midi	at twelve noon
aprés midi	afternoon

Jouons Tous Ensemble © Kathy Williams

School day timetable

	j'ai ...	j'ai ...
à 9 heures		
à 10 heures		
à 11 heures		
à 1 heure		
à 2 heures		
à 3 heures		
à 4 heures		

Chinese counter template

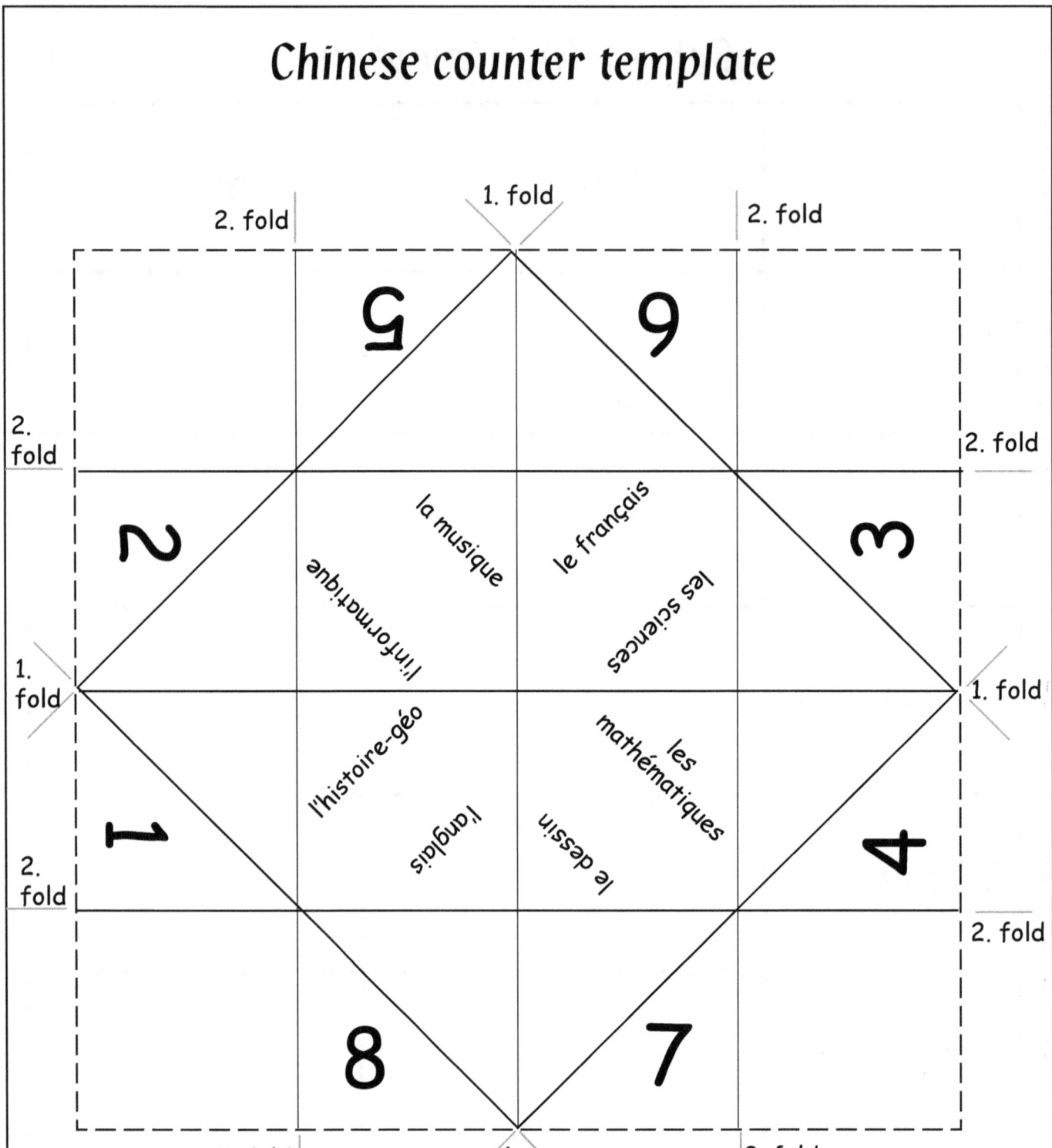

1. Fold corners **back** behind face of paper.
2. Fold corners **inward** to centre.
3. Put your thumb and forefinger of both hands into the back of the resulting square and pinch up into a point.

This page may be photocopied for use by the purchasing institution only.

Jouons Tous Ensemble © Kathy Williams

Like it or not

Board game

Objective
- To practise saying 'j'aime …' and 'je n'aime pas …', while talking about school subjects

Setting up the game
- Pupils play in pairs using an enlarged photocopy of the grid (page 44), a coin, and a different coloured counter each.

Mots clés – Key words
j'aime …	I like …
je n'aime pas …	I don't like …
le français	French
le dessin	art
le sport	PE
l'anglais	English
l'histoire-géo	humanities
la musique	music
l'informatique	ICT
les mathématiques	maths
les sciences	science

How to play the game
1. The players put their counters on 'Commence ici'.
2. They decide who goes first by tossing a coin.
3. Player one tosses the coin – if **heads**, player one moves his/her counter to 'j'aime …' completing the phrase with a school subject, for example, 'j'aime la musique'. If **tails**, player one moves to the 'je n'aime pas …' position instead, and completes the phrase accordingly.
4. Player two then tosses the coin and moves/speaks in the same way. Both players can be on the same place on the grid at the same time.
5. They continue to move across the grid until the first player reaches the last column on the right-hand side of the board. Player two must then throw the **opposite** to player one's last throw, and complete the **opposite** phrase to avoid losing the game. For example, if player one completed the course by throwing heads and said 'J'aime …' then player two has to throw tails to finish, or he has automatically lost the game. If he throws tails then the game is a draw.
6. On completing the game, the players start again (and again) at 'Commence ici', with alternating players starting the game. They should keep a tally of how many games they win. They could play 'best of five' for example.
7. By repeating the game (at a quick pace for older pupils) the language is being continually reinforced. You could make it more challenging by saying that players must not repeat a school subject if their partner has already said it within that game. There are nine school subjects listed in the key words list, so this should be possible.

Extension/variation
- The game can be adapted to practise likes and dislikes of other things e.g. different foods or sports. Note: in some cases you will need to use the plural form, e.g. 'j'aime les pomme**s**' (apples), 'je n'aime pas les banane**s**.'

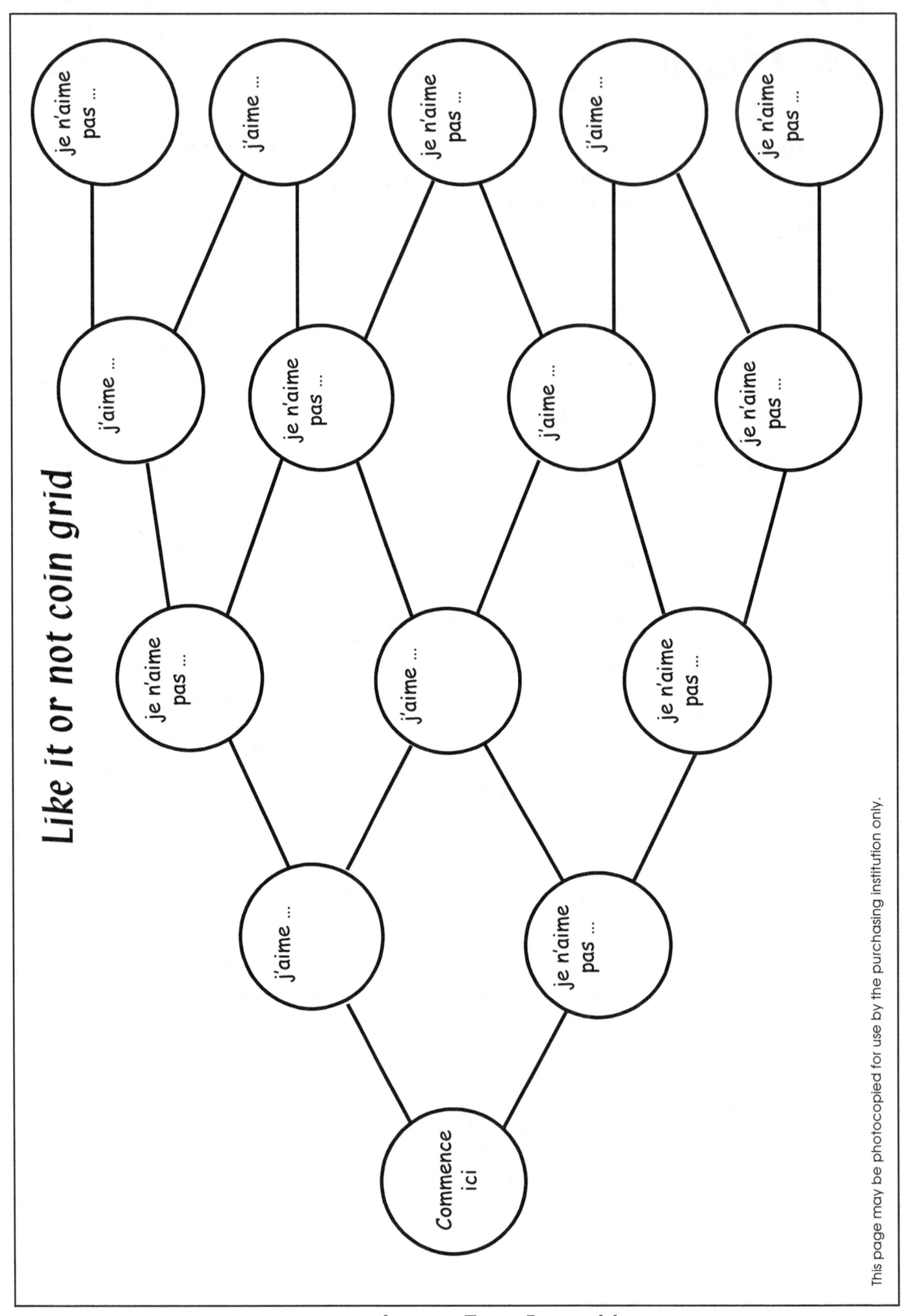

A tour of France

Board game

Objectives
- To practise using transport words
- To practise using 'Je vais à + town'

Mots clés – Key words
je vais à …	I am going to …
Bordeaux, Paris, Marseilles, etc.	
en autobus	by bus
en bateau	by boat
en vélo	by bike
en voiture	by car
par avion	by plane
par le train	by train

Setting up the game
- All players require a map (page 47) each and one die between them, made from the template (page 48). This can be coloured and assembled in advance of the game by the players.
- The same game can be played either in pairs or groups of three or four.

How to play the game
1. Make sure all the players can identify the names of the main towns featured on the map before the game begins.
2. Each player must make a round trip of France, from Paris back to Paris, via the route shown on the map.
3. The players must keep their maps hidden from the view of the other player(s). This is because in the final part of the game, points are lost if two players have chosen the same form of transport for the same leg of the tour.
4. One player starts by rolling the die. He must say aloud the form of transport that he throws, and then quietly decide which part of the route he will make using that form of transport. It can be any leg of the journey that is chosen. For example, if he threw a **train** picture, he could decide to travel by **train** between Lyon and Nice. He makes a note of his choice in the itinerary table below the map, and writes down the points he has scored using the die. Take care to fill in the correct line on the points tally.
5. The next player then throws the die, and makes a choice on his travel itinerary in the same way. The game continues until each player has made a complete route around France. They might have thrown the same picture most of the time and made almost the whole route by car, for example. Or they may have a wide variety of modes of transport in their travel itinerary. If, however, the boat is thrown, it can only be used between Nice and Marseilles. They miss a turn if the Nice to Marseilles leg of the journey has already been filled in.

To score points
- Player one starts by saying in French one of the sections of his journey, for example, 'Je vais à Lyon en voiture.' The other player(s) look(s) at their maps, and if they have used the **car** for this section as well, then they all lose their points for this section. If only the first player has used the **car** here then he keeps his 1 point (on the die the car is worth 1 point).

- The next player then says one of her sections, 'Je vais à Bordeaux par le train.' The other players check their maps and either cross off their **train** and points, or leave other transport choices in place. As before, the player speaking only keeps her points if she is the only player to use the **train** in this part of the tour.
- When the whole route has been discussed, the winner is the player with the most points.

A tour of France

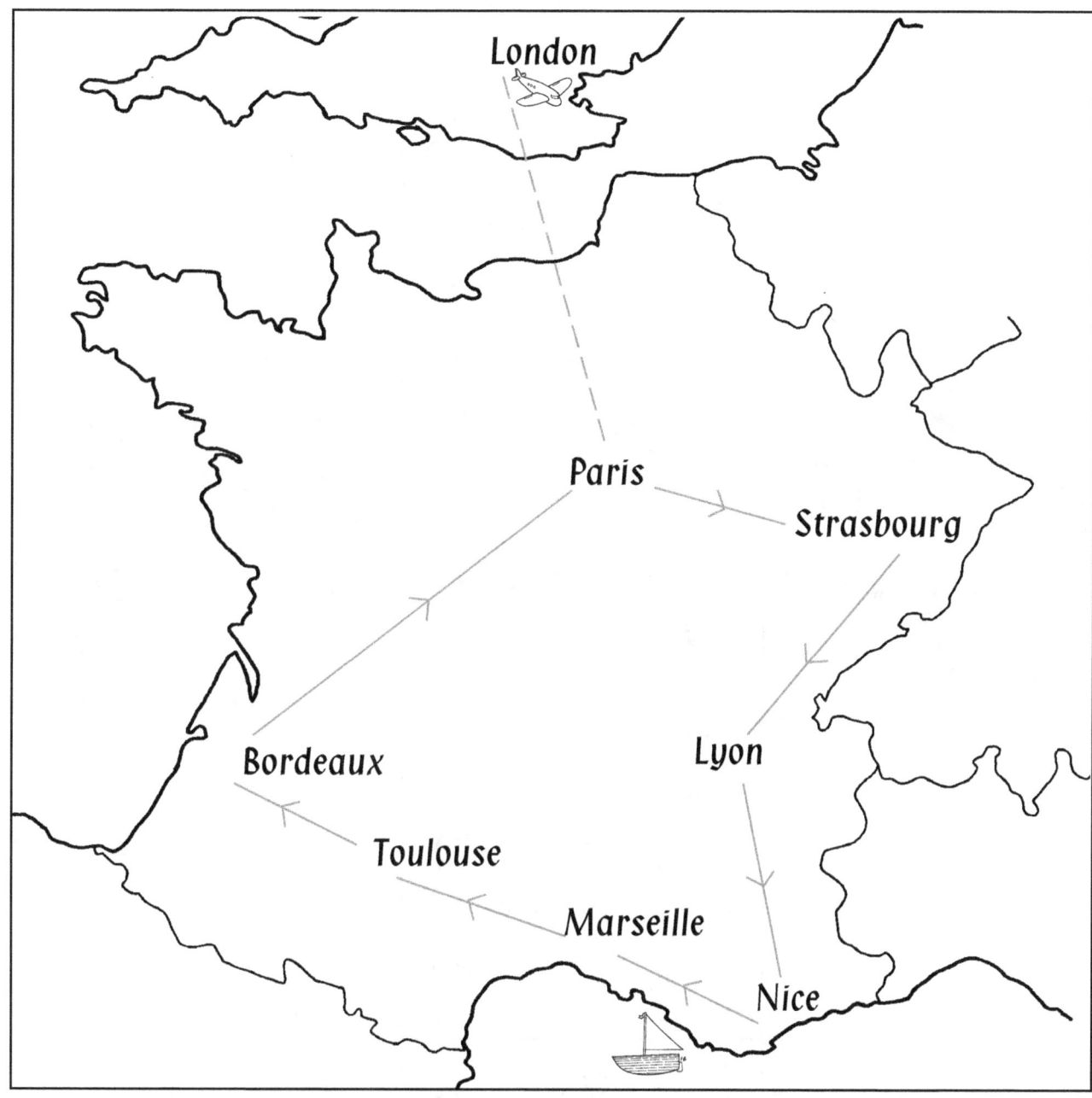

Je vais à Paris	par avion	4	points
Je vais à Strasbourg	....	____	points
Je vais à Lyon	....	____	points
Je vais à Nice	....	____	points
Je vais à Marseille	....	____	points
Je vais à Toulouse	....	____	points
Je vais à Bordeaux	....	____	points
Je vais à Paris	....	____	points

This page may be photocopied for use by the purchasing institution only.

© Kathy Williams Jouons Tous Ensemble

Die template for a tour of France

This page may be photocopied for use by the purchasing institution only.

Jouons Tous Ensemble © Kathy Williams

Quiz corners

Question and answer game/test

Objective
- To assess pupils' knowledge of several areas of language or vocabulary as a 'round-up' of a few weeks' work. The teacher can monitor answers orally during the game, or answers can be written down for the whole class to check at the end of the session.

Setting up the game
- In this game the questions can be in English so that the emphasis is on producing the right language in response, rather than trying to understand the question. Alternatively, as pupils become more knowledgable and confident, both questions and answers can be in French.
- Photocopy and cut out the question vocabulary cards (page 50). Fill in the blanks to practise the particular area(s) of vocabulary that you want to assess. Alternatively, pupils could prepare these in advance for others in the class to use. If you play with just one set of cards, the pupils will have to return them so that other pairs/groups can also answer those questions. Alternatively, if you prepare several sets of cards, pupils could keep the cards and write their answers on them.
- Pupils work in pairs or small groups.

How to play the game
1. Designate the four corners of the classroom as the four 'quiz corners' (or if this is not feasible, four table tops, four trays or boxes). Using four separate areas makes it more interesting than a 'sit-down' test as pupils have to move between the areas and their 'bases'.
2. Name each corner with the first four letters of the French alphabet.
3. Place an equal amount of cards in each of the four corners.
4. Player one chooses a corner at random. Player two has to pick up a card from there and ask player one the question written on the card. Player two then returns the card to the bottom of the pile he/she took it from (if you are playing with just one set of cards).
5. It is now the turn of player two to pick a corner, from which player one has to pick up a question card.
6. If the card chosen has already been answered, the players must still answer the question again before continuing. The fact that some cards may be repeatedly picked up in the attempt to find them all is beneficial as it gives pupils extra practice through repetition.
7. The game can be made competitive by setting a time limit within which the pair/group answering the most questions correctly wins. Alternatively the winning pair/group is the one which completes all the questions first.

Extension/variation
- Each corner could be used to practise a different theme, for example, weather in the 'A' corner, classroom items in the 'B' corner, days of the week in the 'C' corner, etc. Alternatively all the areas could have the same theme.

Corner question vocabulary cards

1. What is ___ in French?	2. What is ___ in French?	3. What is ___ in French?
4. What is ___ in French?	5. What is ___ in French?	6. What is ___ in French?
7. What is ___ in French?	8. What is ___ in French?	9. What is ___ in French?
10. What is ___ in French?	11. What is ___ in French?	12. What is ___ in French?

This page may be photocopied for use by the purchasing institution only.

Jouons Tous Ensemble

Rock, paper, scissors

Question and answer game/test

Objective
- To test vocabulary or spelling using the 'rock, paper, scissors' hand game – more fun than writing down answers to a list of questions! (It can be used to practise any language area.)

Mots clés – Key words

rocher (m)	rock
papier (m)	paper
ciseaux (m, pl)	scissors

Setting up the game
- You can use the cards from 'quiz corners' (page 50) and the spelling cards (page 52). You will need two types of questions – ones which ask for an **oral response**, e.g. 'What is the French word for "cheese"?' and ones which ask the players to **spell** a word, e.g. 'Spell the word for "cheese" in French'. Alternatively questions can be in French, e.g. 'Quel est le mot pour "cheese"?' or 'Ecris "cheese" en français'.
- Players sit in pairs around a table with the question cards in two piles in the middle. They need paper to record scores and for written responses.

How to play the game
1. On the count of three in French they each put out one hand, with the hand made into one of three shapes – **rock** which is the fist clenched into a ball-shape, **paper** which is a flat hand palm downwards, or **scissors** which is the forefinger and middle finger opening and closing (like scissors). If you wish, you could use the French words for 'rock, paper, scissors' (see key words).
2. A player wins the round in the following ways:
    - 'paper' beats 'rock'
    - 'rock' beats 'scissors'
    - 'scissors' beats 'paper'
3. If both players have chosen the same hand shape, then there is no winner for that round and they must play again.
4. Whoever wins a round answers a question.
    - If he won using 'paper', his opponent asks him to **write down** a word.
    - If he won using 'rock', he has to **answer a question orally.**
    - If he won using 'scissors' he can cut his opponent's score back by one point, or he can opt for a question that his opponent chooses.
5. Answering questions correctly will get 2 points, incorrectly 0 points.
6. The winner is the player who has the most points at the end of a time limit, or when all the questions have been used up, whichever is most suitable.

Extension/variation
- Without using written question cards or point scoring, this game works well as a warm-up, a way of players testing each other orally on any subject they wish. It also works well as a time filler at the end of a lesson. Players do the 'rock, paper, scissors' actions and the winner answers questions as before, but they could be anything thought up by their partner, or from a particular theme or vocabulary list.

© Kathy Williams *Jouons Tous Ensemble*

Spelling cards

1. How do you spell _____ in French?	2. How do you spell _____ in French?	3. How do you spell _____ in French?
4. How do you spell _____ in French?	5. How do you spell _____ in French?	6. How do you spell _____ in French?
7. How do you spell _____ in French?	8. How do you spell _____ in French?	9. How do you spell _____ in French?
10. How do you spell _____ in French?	11. How do you spell _____ in French?	12. How do you spell _____ in French?

This page may be photocopied for use by the purchasing institution only.

www.ingramcontent.com/pod-product-compliance
Lightning Source LLC
Chambersburg PA
CBHW081435300426
44108CB00016BA/2376